Instructor's Manual and Test Bank for Galliano's

Gender
Crossing Boundaries

Carie Forden
Clarion University

THOMSON

WADSWORTH

Australia • Canada • Mexico • Singapore • Spain • United Kingdom • United States

Printed in the United States of America
1 2 3 4 5 6 7   05 04 03 02 01

Printer: Edwards Brothers

0-534-24754-7

For more information about our products,
contact us at:
Thomson Learning Academic Resource Center
1-800-423-0563

For permission to use material from this text,
contact us by:
Phone: 1-800-730-2214
Fax: 1-800-731-2215
Web: http://www.thomsonrights.com

Asia
Thomson Learning
5 Shenton Way #01-01
UIC Building
Singapore 068808

Australia
Nelson Thomson Learning
102 Dodds Street
South Street
South Melbourne, Victoria 3205
Australia

Canada
Nelson Thomson Learning
1120 Birchmount Road
Toronto, Ontario M1K 5G4
Canada

Europe/Middle East/South Africa
Thomson Learning
High Holborn House
50/51 Bedford Row
London WC1R 4LR
United Kingdom

Latin America
Thomson Learning
Seneca, 53
Colonia Polanco
11560 Mexico D.F.
Mexico

Spain
Paraninfo Thomson Learning
Calle/Magallanes, 25
28015 Madrid, Spain

Preface

This instructor's manual has been developed for use with Grace Galliano's *Gender: Crossing Boundaries*. This manual includes:

♦ The learning objectives and summary from the text.

♦ A lecture suggestion for each chapter. The lectures are designed to bring greater depth to material discussed in the text, or to provide information on a topic that was not discussed in the text but is relevant to the chapter.

♦ Several activity and discussion suggestions for each chapter, with at least one of these tied to the text's *Zoom and Enlarge*, *ABCs of Gender*, or *Slide Show* features.

♦ A paper assignment for each chapter.

♦ One or two InfoTrac exercises for each chapter. These exercises are designed to help students become familiar with this reference resource while they explore chapter topics in greater depth. All of the exercises are to be used with the Expanded Academic ASAP collection.

♦ At least 25 multiple choice questions for each chapter. For each question, I have included the corresponding learning objective to assist you with item selection. I have also included the page number from the text so you can easily find the information on which the item was based.

♦ At least 10 short answer questions for each chapter. These are designed to be answered in a paragraph or less.

♦ At least 3 essay questions for each chapter.

I hope you find this instructor's manual helps you develop an exciting and challenging class for you and your students. I welcome any comments or suggestions you may wish to share with me (cforden@clarion.edu).

Carie Forden, Ph.D.
Department of Psychology
Clarion University of Pennsylvania

Table of Contents

Chapter 1: Thinking About Sex and Gender

Chapter 2: Studying Gender

Chapter 3: Theories of Gender

Chapter 4: Gender and the Body

Chapter 5: Life Span Gender Development

Chapter 6: Gender and Relationships

Chapter 7: Gender as Social Performance

Chapter 8: Gender and Sexuality

Chapter 9: Gender and Education

Chapter 10: Gender and Work

Chapter 11: Gender and Physical Health

Chapter 12: Gender and Mental Health

Chapter 13: Gender and the Media

Chapter 14: Gender and Power

Chapter 15: Gender and the Future

Chapter 1
Thinking About Sex and Gender

Learning Objectives

1. List and describe 10 components of the concept of gender.

2. Distinguish between the concepts of sex and gender, elaborating on the distinction between *sex differences* and *gender differences.*

3. Offer five reasons for studying the psychology of gender.

4. Explain why, in spite of a major methodological flaw, a cross-cultural perspective on gender is both theoretically useful and personally practical.

5. Compare the sources of gender-related knowledge for the layperson versus those of the gender scholar.

6. Explain the problematic aspects of the term *race* in describing groups and group differences.

7. Explain the problematic aspects of the term *differences* in describing the behaviors of women.

8. Explain the problematic aspects of relying on *individual experience* in attempting to understand gender.

9. List and describe eight themes that will characterize the presentation of the psychology of gender in this text.

Summary

♦ Psychologists can identify and explain at least 10 components of gender.

♦ The term *sex* refers to a biological classification, superficially based on genital appearance. The term *gender* refers to those behaviors and characteristics considered appropriate for the women and men of a particular society.

♦ There is an important and dynamic relationship between certain biological factors determined by one's sex and the socially constructed phenomenon of gender.

♦ Psychologists and other social scientists often make a distinction between *sex differences* versus *gender differences*, but this is sometimes problematic.

♦ There are many good reasons for a formal study of gender, and these relate to commonly asked questions about men and women in our society.

♦ There are many advantages in taking a global perspective on gender. A rationale for a cross-cultural and multicultural perspective is the powerful influence of culture on so many aspects of social behavior. Cultural awareness is both enriching and of practical benefit.

♦ The most general definition of culture involves the sharing of minds. Cultures may be distinguished along the dimension of individualism/collectivism. Lack of representativeness is a major weakness of contemporary cross-cultural psychological research.

♦ Scientific books and journals relating to gender and cultural psychology are important resources for the gender scholar.

♦ Three important issues surround the study of gender. These include the issue of race and ethnicity, the issue of differences, and the issue of the validity of individual experience.

♦ In this text, eight themes will permeate the organization and presentation of the many facets of gender. These include gender as largely a social construction, gender as a lifelong process, a multidisciplinary approach to studying gender, gender as a dynamic process, gender as both a psychosocial phenomenon and as a power arrangement, gender roles as both freeing and constraining the individual, and gender as enmeshed in various social institutions (the family, religion, and so on).

In-Class Activities

Lecture Suggestion:

Lecture: Individualism, Collectivism and Gender

The text describes how cultures can be described as individualistic or collectivistic You may wish to give an example of how this cultural difference can affect gender and gender roles. One such example is marriage:

While marriage in individualistic cultures is seen as involving two individuals, in collectivistic culture marriage occurs between families—a whole extended family "marries" another extended family. Arranged marriages are much more common in collectivism. When considering a potential partner, people in individualistic cultures ask, "what does my heart say?" while those in collectivistic cultures ask "what will other people say?" (Triandis, 1994).

According to Dion and Dion (1993), psychological intimacy in a marriage is more important for marital satisfaction and personal well-being in individualistic societies. In collectivistic societies, other family connections (for example, with parents, in-laws, children) serve as a primary source of intimacy. In a study of arranged marriages in India, it was found that "a sense of lifelong commitment and cultural tradition" was more likely to be related to satisfaction in marriage than "a desire for emotional excitement."

Dion and Dion also make the point that while psychological intimacy in marriage is emphasized in individualistic societies, some aspects of individualism make this intimacy more difficult to achieve. In one study for example, individuals who scored high on a measure of psychological individualism were less likely to report caring, need, and trust of their partners, and were more likely to view "love as a game." Further, Dion and Dion argue that gender may also contribute to the level of psychological intimacy in a marriage. The distinction between individualistic and collectivistic societies is similar to the distinctions made by some feminist psychologists (e.g., Nancy Chodorow, Jean Baker Miller) who see women as constructing a relational self while men construct an autonomous self. This may mean that women have a greater interest in and capacity for psychological intimacy in a marriage. While both men and women in individualistic societies may desire psychological intimacy in marriage, gender-related differences in construal of the self may make it more difficult for men to provide such intimacy to their wives.

References:

Dion, K.K. & Dion, K.L. (1993). Individualistic and collectivistic perspectives on gender and the cultural context of love and intimacy. *Journal of Social Issues, 49* (3), 53-63.

Triandis, H.C. (1994). *Culture and social behavior.* New York: McGraw-Hill, Inc.

Discussion/Activity Suggestions:

1. *Zoom and Enlarge Activity: What is Gender?* Ask your students to take out a piece of paper and write down their definition or description of what the term *gender* means. When they are finished, collect their papers and redistribute them to the class (it doesn't matter if someone ends up with their own paper). Have the students get into groups of five and read the definitions. Ask them to classify the definitions according to the 10 components of the concept of gender. Have the groups report their findings and ask the class the following questions: Which components of the concept of gender were used the most often? Were there any components that were not included in the definitions? Did any of the definitions seem to apply more to sex differences than to gender differences? You may then wish to reconvene the groups and ask each group to come up with a new definition of gender.

2. *Slide Show Activity: Gender Relations Across Cultures.* Divide students into small groups and ask them to write a vignette of a conflict stemming from one of the cultural differences in gender-related behavior described in Box 1.3.

3. *Discussion:* Ask your students to describe the ways that gender roles have constrained them. Then, ask for examples of the ways gender roles have freed them. Finally, ask them if life would be easier if there were no gender roles.

4. *Discussion:* Have your students discuss Galliano's preference for using the term *ethnicity* rather than *race*. Do they agree with her? This will probably be a particularly lively discussion if you have an ethnically diverse group of students.

Paper Assignment

Gender Autobiography: Have students write their autobiography from the perspective of gender, in other words, "My Life as a Male" or "My Life as a Female". Suggest that they use the 10 components of gender to assist them in thinking of the ways their lives have been shaped by gender.

InfoTrac Exercises

Both of these exercises are designed to introduce students to the InfoTrac on-line library:

1. Table 1.1 lists journals that often contain reports of gender-related research. Ask students to find which of these journals are available through InfoTrac. Have them choose a current issue of one of these journals and report on the topics that are addressed.

2. To give students some practice in tracking down a citation, ask them to go to InfoTrac and look up one of the references cited in chapter one.

Test Bank for Chapter 1

Multiple Choice Questions

1. Components of the concept of gender, Obj. 1, p. 3, ans. a

The term "gender"
a. refers to the sum of the observable differences between women and men.
b. refers to a biological classification based on genital appearance.
c. is becoming less useful as males and females become more alike.
d. is mainly used when describing similarities between men and women.

2. Components of the concept of gender, Obj. 1, p. 3-6, ans. d

Which of the following is NOT one of the components of the concept of gender?
a. your inner sense of who you are
b. a set of socially constructed roles
c. a system of power relationships in a society
d. a set of unmodifiable mental potentials

3. Components of the concept of gender, Obj. 1, p. 3, ans. c

When asked to complete the statement "I am...," Matt says "I am a man." This demonstrates:
a. the power of gender stereotypes.
b. a gender proscription.
c. the centrality of gender to self-concept.
d. that gender is more important to men than to women.

4. Components of the concept of gender, Obj. 1, p. 5, ans. b

Which of the following is NOT true of gender?
a. People evaluate themselves and others based on gender ideals.
b. People tend to apply the dualistic concept of gender only to humans.
c. People always act out gender roles in interactions with others.
d. Gender represents the first and most basic social learning about what people are.

5. Components of the concept of gender, Obj. 1, p. 6, ans. c

In the United States, a woman of even the highest status cannot safely walk the streets or roads alone at night. This is an example of
a. a gender stereotype.
b. the role gender plays in self-identity.
c. gender as a system of power relationships.
d. gender as a social category.

6. Distinguish between the concepts of sex and gender, Obj. 2, p. 7, ans. b

Which of the following statements is true of the relationship between sex and gender?
a. Sex and gender are almost completely unrelated.
b. Gender is a social construction that is related to a biological foundation.
c. Sex is the unalterable part of gender.
d. Gender refers to biological potentials while sex refers to environmental influences.

7. Distinguish between the concepts of sex and gender, Obj. 2, p. 7, ans. a

The ability of female breast tissue to produce milk under normal hormonal conditions is an example of:
a. a sex difference.
b. a gender difference.
c. neither a sex nor a gender difference.
d. it has not yet been determined if this is a sex difference or a gender difference.

8. Distinguish between the concepts of sex and gender, Obj. 2, p. 7, ans. a

Which statement accurately describes the influence of environmental factors on biology?
a. Environments and experiences can modify brains and hormonal systems.
b. The biological foundation of gender is infinitely modifiable.
c. Nervous systems cannot be altered by social or experiential factors.
d. Biological potentials build on a social foundation.

9. Five reasons for studying the psychology of gender, Obj. 3, p. 8, ans. c

When Florence Denmark called for "the engendering of psychology," she meant that
a. more women should participate in the field of psychology.
b. that men should be included in the study of gender issues.
c. that psychology should recognize that almost all human behavior occurs in a gendered context.
d. that psychologists should replace the term "sex differences" with the term "gender differences".

10. Five reasons for studying the psychology of gender, Obj. 3, p. 8, ans. b

Which of the following is NOT true of the study of gender?
a. It is valuable to study gender if you wish to understand more about who you are likely to become.
b. It is valuable to study gender because when we look around the world, we see that gender roles and
   gender expectations are remaining unchanged.
c. It is valuable to study gender because your understanding of gender issues may lead you to support or
   object to public policies regarding public health and crime.
d. It is valuable to study gender because it is crucial to any field in which dealing with people is a major
   component.

11. Explain why a cross-cultural perspective on gender is useful, Obj. 4. p. 10, ans. a

When it comes to how prescribed blueprints for gender are actually lived out
a. in very traditional societies, violations of gender roles are relatively frequent.
b. the majority of people conform absolutely to the gender prescriptions of their society.
c. in North American culture, women are more likely to be severely punished for gender role violations.
d. in traditional societies, violations of gender roles are relatively rare.

12. Explain why a cross-cultural perspective on gender is useful, Obj. 4, p. 10 ans. d

Which of the following is NOT true of the cross-cultural study of gender?
a. It can help you refute arguments about the essential differences between women and men.
b. It allows you to relish and celebrate the gender constructions of other societies.
c. It helps us step outside our own society's prescribed blueprint for gender.
d. Psychology has always taken a cross-cultural perspective on gender.

13. Explain why a cross-cultural perspective on gender is useful, Obj. 4, p. 11, ans. b

In a collectivist society,
a. personal needs and goals take precedence.
b. members see themselves as fundamentally connected with others.
c. the needs of the group may be sacrificed to satisfy the needs of the individual.
d. members tend to see themselves as separate and autonomous.

14. Explain why a cross-cultural perspective on gender is useful, Obj. 4, p. 11, ans. a

The story of David and Melissa illustrates:
a. that knowledge of multicultural gender norms can come in handy.
b. that men and women have difficulties communicating with each other.
c. that men and women are more alike than different.
d. that gender norms are shared across cultures.

15. Compare the sources of gender-related knowledge, Obj. 5. p. 12, ans. c

The source of gender-related knowledge for most people is_____, but psychologists tend to rely on_____ to learn about gender.
a. newspaper stories, interviews
b. hearsay, personal experience
c. personal experience, scientific studies
d. scientific studies, cross-cultural research

16. Explain the problematic aspects of the term *race*, Obj. 6, p. 13, ans. c

Arranging data by race
a. helps clarify and organize data.
b. avoids stereotyping.
c. can be confusing and misleading.
d. is more accurate than arranging data by ethnicity.

17. Explain the problematic aspects of the term *race*, Obj. 6, p. 13, ans. d

The term *ethnicity* refers to
a. a group of people who share a religion.
b. a group of people who share an appearance.
c. a group of people who share a culture.
d. all of the above.

18. Explain the problematic aspects of the term *race*, Obj. 6, p. 13, ans. d

Which of the following statements regarding the terms "race" and "ethnicity" is true?
a. Ethnicity is often erroneously seen as referring to a biological classification.
b. Race is a clear and scientific term.
c. Race is generally understood to be a social construction.
d. Ethnicity appears to more accurately convey useful information than race.

19. Explain the problematic aspects of the term *difference* in describing women, Obj. 7, p. 14, ans. c

In a study of play behavior, it was found that all of the girls and most of the boys engaged in a low or medium level of rough and tumble play. However, a few boys who engaged in a very high level of rough and tumble play, pushed the average for boys way up. Based on this study we can conclude:
a.   boys play more roughly than girls do
b.   girls play more roughly than boys do
c.   levels of rough and tumble play are about the same for most boys and girls
d.   male hormones influence boys to play more roughly than girls

20. Explain the problematic aspects of the term *difference* in describing women, Obj. 7, p. 14, ans. a

A friend tells you that she has learned that women are more depressed than men. What do you say?
a. "That may just be a statistical artifact."
b. "You're right!"
c. "No, men are more depressed than women."
d. "Yes, and men are more antisocial than women."

21. Explain the problematic aspects of relying on *individual experience*, Obj. 8, p. 15, ans. b

When it comes to relying on your personal experience to understand gender, you should keep in mind
a. that individual experience should be used to negate the accuracy of more general statements.
b. that your individual experience may not be typical.
c. that you are unlikely to experience your gender norms as universally human.
d. that individual experience is always representative of the larger picture.

22. Explain the problematic aspects of relying on *individual experience*, Obj. 8, p. 15, ans. d

Which of the following statements regarding generalizations about gender is true?
a. Generalizations about gender apply to all men and women.
b. Generalizations cannot be made about gender because everyone is different.
c. Generalizations about gender are not particularly useful.
d. Generalizations about gender can be accurate even if they don't apply to you.

23. List and describe eight themes that characterize this text, Obj. 9, p. 16, ans. a

Which of the following statements regarding the construction of gender is true?
a. Gender constructions are dynamic.
b. Gender is mainly a biological construction.
c. Economic forces are not important in the construction of gender.
d. Gender constructions affect us primarily during childhood.

24. List and describe eight themes that characterize this text, Obj. 9, p. 16, ans. c

Gender roles
a. constrain individuals.
b. free individuals.
c. both constrain and free individuals.
d. neither constrain nor free individuals.

25. List and describe eight themes that characterize this text, Obj. 9, p. 16, ans. b

Which of the following is NOT a major theme of the text?
a. Although sex is determined by biological factors, gender is mainly a social construction.
b. Because gender impacts primarily on the individual, it is best studied by psychologists.
c. Individuals construct and maintain gender throughout their lifetimes.
d. Egalitarian gender arrangements are more desirable and beneficial.

Short-Answer Questions

26. Explain the idea that gender is a core aspect of internal self-identity.

27. Give examples of a gender prescription and a gender proscription that you have experienced.

28. Distinguish between the concepts of sex and gender.

29. How can understanding gender help you make better decisions as a citizen?

30. What is the difference between a multicultural perspective on gender and a cross-cultural perspective on gender?

31. Define *culture*.

32. What is a weakness of contemporary cross-cultural psychology?

33. Distinguish between the term "race" and the term "ethnicity."

34. What is the problem with only reporting the averages for males and females in studies that look at gender differences?

35. What does it mean to say that "gender is dynamic?"

Essay Questions

36. Why is it useful to take a cross-cultural approach to the study of gender?

37. Why does Galliano claim that the term *ethnicity* seems to more accurately convey useful information than the term *"race"*?

38. If a friend asked you why he should take a gender class, what would you tell him?

39. How will you respond when you share what you have learned about gender with someone and they say "that does not apply to me, nor to the people I know!"

40. What does it mean to say that gender is mainly a social construction?

Chapter 2
Studying Gender

Learning Objectives

1. Describe the basic steps of the scientific method, and explain how they are related to three important philosophical assumptions regarding the nature of reality.

2. Referring to the earliest psychologists, explain the relationship among conceptualizations of group differences, evolutionary theory, gender, and ethnicity.

3. Summarize three conceptualizations of gender as envisioned by psychologists, emphasizing the strengths and weaknesses of the concept of androgyny.

4. Define the term *gender stereotype* and summarize the findings relevant to understanding the importance of gender stereotypes.

5. Summarize the strengths and weaknesses of the case study, observation, and survey research, emphasizing the particular challenge presented by multicultural and cross-cultural research.

6. Summarize the strengths and weaknesses of the developmental, correlational, and experimental approaches, emphasizing the problems of causation and ex post facto studies.

7. Describe how meta-analyses are carried out, and explain why meta-analysis is a useful method for studying gender differences.

8. Contrast the qualitative approach with more traditional quantitative methods.

9. Explain the impact of the criticisms raised by feminist psychologists regarding the study of women and gender.

10. Contrast the current study of men as explicitly gendered with more traditional approaches, and then briefly summarize eight important issues in studying men and masculinity.

11. Explain why the issue of sexual orientation is important in studying gender.

12. Explain why cross-cultural and multicultural approaches are important in studying gender.

13. Summarize the main tenets of the social constructionist approach to gender.

14. Briefly describe two or more important problems to consider in studying gender.

Summary

♦ The philosophical concepts of empiricism, materialism, and positivism are at the core of the scientific approach to studying gender. Basically, the scientific method involves collecting data according to particular rules, analyzing data, and then interpreting that data. The earliest psychologists were heavily influenced by misinterpretations of evolutionary theory in their approach to understanding human differences. This resulted in an androcentric and ethnocentric psychology. Feminist psychologists have confronted the sexism and ethnocentrism that permeated the concepts and methodology of traditional psychology.

♦ The study of gender stereotypes has been useful in understanding the distortions that surround the psychology of gender.

♦ The case study, observation, developmental approaches, and surveys are all methods for describing gender-related behavior and mental processes. Each method has its own strengths and weaknesses.

♦ Although studies of the correlations among variables permit the prediction of group behavior, they do not permit conclusions regarding causality. The experiment is a powerful research method that permits statements of causality. The dangers of *ex post facto* studies and overattribution to biological causes must be considered.

♦ Meta-analysis is a valuable method for the study of gender differences.

♦ Qualitative studies facilitate the understanding of gender-related processes and experiences, but certain weaknesses are inherent in this approach.

♦ Over the last several decades, important new research on men as explicitly gendered has gradually emerged.

♦ Beliefs about the relationship between sexual orientation and gender norms are important issues in the study of gender.

♦ Multicultural psychology focuses on group differences *within* a society. Cross-cultural psychology focuses on both similarities and differences *between* societies.

♦ Multicultural and cross-cultural perspectives are crucial for understanding and appreciating the social construction of gender in human groups. Cultural psychologists emphasize that social norms (such as gender and culture) *guide* but do not *cause* behavior.

♦ Social constructionists have offered strong critiques of positivistic approaches and have pointed out that social reality is often determined by language and power arrangements.

♦ Two additional problems in gender research are the problem of reification and the inherent paradox of gender studies.

In-Class Activities

Lecture Suggestion:

Lecture: The Role of Gender in College Students' Evaluations of Faculty

A study conducted by Bachen, McLoughlin & Garcia (1999) provides a relevant illustration of the effects of gender schemas on the perception and interpretation of behavior. In this study, 486 male and female university students were asked to complete both qualitative and quantitative assessments of their male and female teachers. On the quantitative assessment, female students gave especially high ratings to female professors and comparatively lower ratings to male professors on items designed to measure the qualities of being caring-expressive, interactive, professional-challenging, and organized. Male students on the other hand, did not rate male and female faculty differently.

A qualitative assessment which asked students whether they had "experienced any important differences between male and female faculty in their teaching or approach to them as a student in or out of the classroom," (p. 195) helped to clarify this gender difference in the evaluation of faculty. An analysis of students' responses to this question revealed that the strength of students' gender schemas influenced their assessment of male and female faculty. Both male and female students (particularly female), praised female professors for their approachability, interest in and support for the student, and enthusiasm. These female students had similar nurturing expectations for their male professors and were disappointed when those professors did not meet those needs. Male students however, applied more traditional gender schema to their evaluation of male professors and did not expect those qualities from them, even though nurturing is seen as part of the ideal professor's role.

Traditional gender schema also were apparent in evaluations by a number of males and a smaller number of females who praised male faculty for their ability to provide a rigorous and demanding classroom experience. Female faculty on the other hand, were more likely to be criticized for doing this. In addition, female faculty were more likely to be seen as insecure, intimidated, and ineffective, in other words, not meeting the professional aspects of the ideal professor's role.

Bachen et al. argue that not only may gender schema lead to differential valuing of male and female faculty, it may also lead to differential preferences regarding teaching styles. Faculty and students of each gender may have a common gender schema, which influences their understanding of classroom values, norms and behaviors. Citing the research by Belenky, Clinchy, Goldberger, & Tarule in their book, *Women's Ways of Knowing* (full citation available in text), the authors argue that females may prefer "connected teaching," which emphasizes relationships, valuing of students' experiences, and uncertainty in the learning process. Female students then, may positively evaluate female teachers who share these values and show these behaviors more often. Male students may prefer a more "male" style of teaching, and so may evaluate female professors more negatively .

References:

Bachen, C.M., McLoughlin, M.M., & Garcia, S.S. (1999). Assessing the role of gender in college students' evaluations of faculty. *Communication Education, 48* (3), 193-210.

Discussion/Activity Suggestions:

1. *Zoom and Enlarge Activity: Revealing Gender Stereotypes in the Lab and in Life.* Box 2.1 describes how gender stereotypes can influence the perception and interpretation of behavior in the lab and in life. To give students some first-hand experience with this, show a clip of the *Saturday Night Live* character "Pat." "Pat" demonstrates the power of gender stereotyping by refusing to reveal his/her gender. Ask the students how it feels not to know Pat's gender. How might Pat's behavior be interpreted differently depending upon gender? Why is it funny to have a character whose gender is not revealed?

2. *Zoom and Enlarge Activity: Should Psychologists Study Gender Differences?* Divide students into

small groups and ask them to prepare an argument for or against the study of gender differences using the arguments presented in Box 2.4.

3. *Activity:* Divide students into small groups and assign each group a different method (survey, interview, experiment, observation). Ask the groups to design a study that will test the hypothesis that females are more nurturant than males (or another hypothesis of your choosing). Have each group present their ideas to the class, and discuss the strengths and weaknesses of each design.

4. *Discussion:* The text argues that "one of the most distinctive characteristics of masculinity or manliness is that something significant must be done to transform a male person into a man," (p. 36). Ask students how this transformation occurs in our society--what rituals, achievements, experiences, etc. must a male person go through in order to become a man? Because manhood is something that is achieved, it is also always in danger of being lost. What ways can a man lose his manhood in our society? You may also wish to ask the class if this process is also true for females--is femininity something that must be achieved and can be lost?

Paper Assignment

Research Critique: Ask students to choose an area of gender research and assign them the task of finding four studies on this subject, each of which use a different research methodology (e.g., an experimental study, a qualitative study, a meta-analysis, a survey). Their paper should describe the strengths and weakness of each study's methodology. Which method seems best suited for researching this topic?

InfoTrac Exercise

Using the InfoTrac key term search feature, students can search for examples of the research methods described in this chapter. Using the search terms **gender and case study, gender and observation, gender and survey, gender and experiment, gender and qualitative,** and **gender and meta-analysis** should bring up numerous examples of each method. Ask them to answer the following questions for each study they review: What question was the researcher addressing in this study? What was learned from the study? Was this method an effective way to address this question? Why or why not?

Test Bank for Chapter 2

Multiple Choice Questions

1. Basic steps of the scientific method, Obj. 1, p. 21, ans. b

Which of the following is NOT a philosophical assumption of the scientific approach?
a. materialism
b. essentialism
c. logical positivism
d. materialism

2. Basic steps of the scientific method, Obj. 1, p. 21, ans. d

Empiricism assumes
a. that there must be agreed-on methods for the collection of data on gender.
b. that gender cannot be studied scientifically.
c. that laws govern all processes of nature, including gender.
d. that gender must be directly observable in order to be studied.

3. Early conceptualizations of gender, Obj. 2, p. 22, ans. c

Which of the following statements regarding early psychology and the study of gender is FALSE?
a. Men were seen as very varied, while women were seen as pretty much alike.
b. Educated white men of the upper classes were seen as the highest examples of human evolution.
c. The behavior of men and women was seen as being of equal interest to psychology.
d. Women were seen as inferior, and the basis of this inferiority was biological.

4. Early conceptualizations of gender, Obj. 2, p. 23, ans. a

During the 20th century, a major bias in psychology regarding gender was
a. that white male behavior was the norm against which the behavior of others was compared.
b. that revealed gender differences were generally transformed into female strengths.
c. that the application of evolutionary theory to gender resulted in a focus on gender similarities.
d. that gender roles were unique to white, middle-class people.

5. Summarize three conceptualizations of gender, Obj. 3, p. 25, ans. c

Inge Broverman and her colleagues found that mental health professionals indicated
a. the psychological characteristics of a healthy woman matched those of a healthy man.
b. the psychological characteristics of a healthy person matched those of a healthy woman.
c. the psychological characteristics of a healthy man matched those of a healthy person.
d. the psychological characteristics of a healthy person matched those of an unhealthy man.

6. Summarize three conceptualizations of gender, Obj. 3, p. 7, ans. b

In the Bem Sex-Role Inventory,
a. femininity and masculinity are seen as opposite poles of a single continuum.
b. femininity and masculinity are seen as two separate and independent dimensions of personality.
c. femininity and masculinity are seen as nonoverlapping concepts.
d. femininity and masculinity are seen as somewhat overlapping.

7. Strengths and weaknesses of the concept of androgyny, Obj. 3, p. 25, ans. c

On the Bem Sex-Role Inventory, an androgynous person
a. has a high femininity score and a low masculinity score.
b. has a high masculinity score and a low femininity score.
c. has a high femininity score and a high masculinity score.
d. has a low masculinity score and a low femininity score.

8. Strengths and weaknesses of the concept of androgyny, Obj. 3, p. 25, ans. a

Which of the following is NOT a shortcoming of the concept of *androgyny*?
a. The concept of androgyny has generated a great deal of empirical research.
b. It is not clear whether androgyny is a personality trait or a gender stereotype.
c. Most studies of androgyny are correlational rather than causal.
d. Androgyny theory seems to reinforce dualistic thinking about gender.

9. Define *gender stereotype* and summarize findings on gender stereotyping, Obj. 4, p. 27, ans. b

Stereotypes
a. wield little power.
b. are alive and well in all of us.
c. are more helpful than harmful.
d. are never helpful.

10. Summarize the strengths and weaknesses of case study, observation, and survey research, Obj. 5, p. 28, ans. d

Which of the following is NOT true of case studies?
a. It involves the collection of detailed information about one or more individuals.
b. It allows the researcher to delve into complex issues.
c. It offers no protection against the researcher's personal and professional biases.
d. It requires that the researcher use random assignment.

11. Summarize the strengths and weaknesses of case study, observation, and survey research, Obj. 5, p. 30, ans. b

A strength of survey research is
a. that it involves collecting data about publicly observable behavior.
b. that it facilitates the collection of data from a great many individuals relatively quickly.
c. that participants are likely to respond with socially desirable answers.
d. that survey items are easily applied cross-culturally.

12. Summarize the strengths and weaknesses of developmental, correlational, and experimental approaches, Obj. 6, p. 31, ans. c

Why might researchers prefer to use a *longitudinal* approach to gender research rather than a *cross-sectional* approach?
a. It is less expensive to conduct longitudinal research.
b. Comparable and representative groups can easily be identified.
c. The psychosocial environment influences each generational cohort.
d. The cross-sectional approach is time-consuming.

13. Summarize the strengths and weaknesses of developmental, correlational, and experimental approaches, Obj. 6, p. 32, ans. a

All women research participants score higher on *ubiquitous plasticity* than men do. What can we conclude?
a. This is a gender-related difference.
b. This difference was caused by the gender of the participants.
c. This difference was caused by the sex of the participants.
d. This difference is the result of random assignment.

14. Describe how meta-analyses are carried out, Obj. 7, p. 32, ans. b

Meta-analyses
a. cannot reveal effect size.
b. combine the results of many studies.
c. rely on the researcher's ability to choose only the best studies.
d. should not include unpublished research.

15. Contrast the qualitative approach with quantitative methods, Obj. 8, p. 33, ans. d

Which of the following is an example of qualitative research?
a. A researcher counts the minutes a father spends holding his infant.
b. A researcher develops a questionnaire that asks fathers to rate their experiences on a scale of 1-5.
c. A researcher rates the quality of a father's interactions with his child.
d. A researcher asks a father to talk about what it is like for him to care for his child.

16. Explain the impact of the criticisms raised by feminist psychologists, Obj. 9, p. 35 ans. a

Feminist psychologists have recommended that
a.   there should be a wider representation of research participants to include the experiences of people who are not in the dominant majority group.
b.   when research articles are considered for publication, gender should be identified so that more articles by women will be published.
c.   researchers should take women's behavior as the norm and describe men as deviating from that norm.
d.   researchers who are female should conduct research with women, while male researchers should conduct research with men.

17. Contrast the current study of men with more traditional approaches, Obj. 10, p. 36 ans. c

The traditional masculine gender role
a. allows for the inclusion of some feminine behaviors in a man's public presentation of himself.
b. includes an overemphasis on thought rather than action to solve life's problems.
c. requires constricted overdevelopment of anger and aggression.
d. sees manhood as something that is given at birth.

18. Contrast the current study of men with more traditional approaches, Obj. 10, p. 36 ans. b

What do scholars mean when they say that there are many "masculinities"?
a. Each man has his own unique way of expressing his masculinity.
b. The concept of masculinity varies by culture, ethnicity, social status, and sexual orientation.
c. There are many gender-related issues that surround the study of men and masculinity.
d. Masculinity is so complex a concept, it cannot be captured by just one definition.

19. Explain why issue of sexual orientation is important in studying gender, Obj. 11, p. 14, ans. d

Which of the following statements about sexual orientation and gender is NOT true?
a. Those who engage in erotic behavior with members of their own sex are seen as not being members of their own gender.
b. People still tend to believe that there is a predictable relationship between sexual orientation and adherence to traditional gender roles.
c. Those whose behavior or interests cross the gender line are considered likely to be homosexual.
d. Because homosexuality is becoming more accepted, it is no longer a central component of the social construction of gender roles.

20. Explain why cross-cultural and multicultural approaches are important, Obj. 12, p. 38, ans. a

According to cultural psychologists, norms
a. guide our behavior.
b. cause our behavior.
c. have no effect on our behavior.
d. transform our behavior.

21. Explain why cross-cultural and multicultural approaches are important, Obj. 12, p. 38, ans. d

Multicultural psychology is concerned with
a. group differences based on ethnicity.
b. group differences based on religion.
c. group differences based on language.
d. all of the above.

22. Summarize the main tenets of the social constructionist approach, Obj. 13, p. 39, ans. b

According to the social constructionist perspective, science
a. is value-free and focuses on objective facts.
b. is the enactment of certain Western cultural values.
c. should not be used to study gender.
d. is less biased than it used to be.

23. Summarize the main tenets of the social constructionist approach, Obj. 13, p. 39, ans. c

The assumption that language creates what is real in the world is central to
a. positivism.
b. reification.
c. social constructionism.
d. materialism.

24. Briefly describe two more important problems in studying gender, Obj. 14, p. 39, ans. a

_____ is when a researcher treats an abstract concept as though it was a real thing.
a. Reification
b. Social constructionism
c. Positivism
d. Materialism

25. . Briefly describe two more important problems in studying gender, Obj. 14, p. 39, ans. c

Why is it a paradox for gender researchers to have the ultimate goal of making gender irrelevant to modern society?
a. Because such a goal is impossible to achieve.
b. Because virtually all research on gender differences is merely descriptive.
c. Because gender researchers bring a great deal of attention to the issue of gender through their work.
d. Because egalitarian gender arrangements are not desirable and beneficial.

Short-Answer Questions

26. Describe how early psychologists viewed women.

27. What is a criticism of the concept of *androgyny*?

28. What does it mean to say that "gender and gender differences *may exist primarily in our own perceptions and interpretations of behavior*," (p. 28).

29. What are two weaknesses of survey research?

30. What is the inherent limitation of all correlational studies?

31. Why might a researcher prefer to use a longitudinal approach rather than a cross-sectional approach to studying gender?

32. If an experiment shows a significant gender difference in a behavior, why can't we conclude that gender *caused* this difference?

33. What does it mean to study men "as explicitly gendered individuals?" (p. 36)

34. What are two of the major gender-related issues that surround the study of men?

35. Why is the issue of sexual orientation important in studying gender?

36. What is the central paradox of all gender research?

Essay Questions

38. Use what you have learned about science to challenge Dr. Edward Clarke's conclusions.

39. "Every observer is a gendered individual who lives in a heavily gendered world, and this affects how we perceive and interpret reality,"(p. 29). What are the implications of this statement for conducting research on gender?

40. Should psychologists study gender differences? Why or why not?

Chapter 3
Theories of Gender

Learning Objectives

1. Define the term *theory,* and describe the functions of theories, emphasizing the criteria for a good theory.

2. Briefly summarize how the ancient Greek and later Christian philosophers viewed the basic nature of women and men.

3. Describe the central focus of the biological perspective on gender, explain the core concepts of the evolutionary approach, and evaluate the insights provided by cross-species comparisons.

4. Summarize the strengths and weaknesses of the biological approach to gender.

5. Explain the central concerns of the psychological perspective on gender, and briefly summarize some traditional psychoanalytic approaches to gender, and feminist reinterpretations of this perspective.

6. List and explain the core concepts of the social learning approach to gender acquisition, and contrast this with the cognitive-developmental and social-cognitive approaches, emphasizing Bem's gender schema theory.

7. Summarize feminist criticisms of traditional psychological theories of gender, and describe the two general approaches taken by feminist gender researchers.

8. Describe the rationale and core concepts of the gender-in-context perspective.

9. Summarize the strengths and weaknesses of the psychological perspective regarding gender.

10. Explain the central concerns of the traditional sociological perspective on gender, and contrast that with the more feminist approach of social role theory.

11. Summarize the strengths and weaknesses of the sociological perspective regarding gender.

12. Summarize the central concerns of the anthropological approach to gender, and evaluate its strengths and weaknesses.

13. Summarize the core concepts of one Eastern approach to nature (and gender).

Summary

♦ A scientific theory is a set of ideas or concepts that organizes knowledge about some phenomenon. The usefulness of a theory determines its quality. People can use theories to generate new questions and to interpret new data.

♦ Good (useful) theories are empirically based, parsimonious, comprehensive, noncontradictory, testable, practical, and acceptable to other experts.

- Biological approaches emphasize the influence of genes and hormones on the brain and nervous system. Evolutionary approaches emphasize gender as differential reproductive strategies for males and females. Cross-species comparisons reveal a wide array of male-female relationships.

- Psychological theories deal with issues of gender role acquisition, maintenance, and application in personality development and interpersonal interaction. Psychoanalytic theories emphasize anatomy and identification. Social learning theories emphasize reinforcement, punishment, vicarious reinforcement, observation, and modeling as the mechanisms for gender role acquisition and maintenance.

- Cognitive-developmental theorists take a counterintuitive, stage approach to gender identity formation and gender role acquisition. Gender schema theory emphasizes the formation of mental frameworks (schemas) that guide and direct behavior.

- Feminist approaches may be classified along the dimensions of empiricist/minimalists to feminist standpoint/maximalist.

- The gender-in-context perspective approaches gender as existing, not within a person, but within a socially constructed transaction between and among individuals.

- Social role theory is an example of a sociological approach to gender. So-called gender differences are viewed as emerging from the typical superior-subordinate roles enacted by women and men. Eventually men and women come to be seen as possessing the qualities their respective roles require.

- Anthropological approaches describe and compare whole societies regarding gendered behavior. Although all societies make some distinction between the roles of women and men, they differ regarding the contents of these roles, the rights and power of each gender, and the social and economic value placed on the activities of men and women.

- The Chinese principle of yin and yang emphasizes the maintenance of balance and harmony between related aspects of all things in the universe, including the relationship between women and men.

In-Class Activities

Lecture Suggestion:

Lecture: Raising Gender-Aschematic Children

Examples of how theories can be applied to everyday life may raise students' level of interest and should help them better understand the theories. One such example is Sandra Bem's (1983) discussion of how to raise gender-aschematic children.

According to Bem, raising gender-aschematic children involves several steps:

1. Delay children's exposure to cultural messages about gender through the following: eliminating gender stereotyping in the parents' own behavior (e.g., both parents drive, both cook, both change diapers); eliminating gender stereotyping in the choices offered to the children (e.g. regardless of gender, each child is given dolls and trucks, pink and blue clothes, both boy and girl friends); and exposing children to adults who are in nontraditional occupations (e.g. female truck drivers, male nurses). Parents can also

censor books and television programs that portray cultural gender differences, and find (or create through doctoring) materials that do not convey gender stereotypes.

2. In addition to teaching children what sex is not (cultural differences between the genders), they must also be taught what sex is (biological differences). Children should be taught that gender matters only in relation to reproduction and anatomy. For example, when Bem's children asked if someone was a male or a female, her reply was that she couldn't tell without seeing if the person had a penis or a vagina.

3. Because a child will eventually confront a world where the gender schema is pervasive, it is necessary to provide alternatives to the gender schema, which can be used to organize and understand gender-related information. Three alternative schemas can be taught: a) the individual differences schema--that there is more variation between individuals than there is between groups. For example, if a child says that only men are doctors, the parent can point out that although some doctors are men, there are also women that the child knows who are doctors; b) the cultural relativism schema--that different people believe different things, and that such differences are the norm. This schema will help a child when it becomes clear that they have beliefs about gender that differ from their peers. It also makes it possible to then expose the child to literature and media that feature gender stereotypes, because the child can be told that the person who wrote the literature or created the television program had a different view of gender which does not have to influence their own view; c) the sexism schema--an understanding of both the history and current status of sex discrimination. This schema will enable the child to understand why the genders seem so different in our society (e.g., why there hasn't been a female president, why fathers don't stay home with children), even though they are not!

References:

Bem, S.L. (1983). Gender schema theory and its implications for child development: raising gender-aschematic children in a gender-schematic society. *Signs: Journal of Women in Culture and Society, 8* (4), 598-611.

Discussion/Activity Suggestions:

1. *ABC's of Gender Activity: Applying Theory to Explain Behavior.* Box 3.2 contains an exercise that should work well in class. Divide students into groups and assign each group one or two of the listed theories. Ask the groups to use their theories to explain the behaviors described. When everyone is finished, go through each of the behavior descriptions and have the groups report to the class on their interpretations. Which theory seems to do the best job of explaining behavior?

2. *Activity: Students' Theories of Gender.* Prior to beginning the chapter on theories of gender, ask students either individually or in groups, to describe their own theories of gender by writing down their answers to these three questions: 1) What gender differences are there (if any) in the behavior and mental processes of men and women, 2) How do you explain these differences or lack of differences? 3) How do we learn our gender identity? After they have studied the theories of gender, ask them to identify which theory or theories is the most similar to theirs, and which theory is the most different. Did they change their minds about their own theory of gender through learning about other theories?

3. *Discussion:* Ask students whether or not they live in a highly gender-schematic society. Does our society emphasize the distinctions between women and men, boys and girls? How? Are there cultural differences in the strength and content of gender-schemas in our society?

4. *Zoom and Enlarge Discussion: Cross-Species Comparisons.* Use the descriptions of primate behaviors to engage students in a discussion of the value of cross-species comparisons. Can we learn something about gender by examining the relationships between males and females of those species most closely related to our own? Why or why not?

Paper Assignment

Position Paper: Ask students to choose one of the following positions and write a paper in support of that position using what they have learned about theories of gender to support their argument. Position 1: Women are more suited to parenting than men. Position 2: Women and men are equally suited to parenting. Position 3: Men and women are psychologically different. Position 4: Men and women are psychologically similar. Position 5: It is possible to make significant changes in gender roles. Position 6: It is almost impossible to make significant changes in gender roles.

InfoTrac Exercise

Ask students to use InfoTrac to find research that supports or refutes one of the theoretical perspectives outlined in the text. The following key words should bring up a number of articles: **gender schema**, **gender-in-context**, **gender constancy** (for cognitive developmental theory), **Carol Gilligan** (for maximalist perspective), and **social role theory**. Ask students to use the research to evaluate the theory by answering the following questions: How did the researchers test the theory? What were the key findings of this research? How do these findings either support or refute the theory?

Test Bank for Chapter 3

Multiple Choice Questions

1. Define the term *theory*, and describe the functions of theories, Obj. 1, p. 44, ans. a

A theory
a. organizes observations and scientific findings.
b. cannot generally be used to understand practical situations.
c. is designed to be narrowly applied.
d. should not be used as the basis for how we interpret observations or data

2. Define the term *theory*, and describe the functions of theories, Obj. 1, p. 45, ans. c

Which of the following is NOT a quality of a useful theory?
a. There is good empirical evidence to support the theory.
b. The theory does not contradict itself as new findings accumulate.
c. The theory is as complex as possible.
d. The theory is testable by scientific methods.

3. Briefly summarize how Greek and Christian philosophers view gender, Obj. 2, p. 45, ans. b

Aristotle argued that
a. there should be unity and equality between the sexes
b. in all ways that mattered, women were inferior to men
c. deep relationships were possible only between women
d. the ideal man developed the feminine side of his nature

4. Describe the central focus of the biological perspective on gender, Obj. 3, p. 46, ans. a

Which of the following statements regarding biological influence on gender is true?
a. Brain organization may change in response to psychological or cultural influences.
b. There is no clear sex difference in hypothalamic, pituitary, and gonadal functioning.
c. Over the decades, the list of biological sex differences has become longer.
d. The higher on the evolutionary scale, the more behavior is influenced by biology.

5. Explain the core concepts of the evolutionary approach, Obj. 3, p. 47, ans. a

Which theory of gender argues that traditional gender roles are the result of adaptation?
a. Evolutionary theory
b. Psychoanalytic theory
c. Social role theory
d. Gender schema theory

6. Summarize the strengths and weaknesses of the biological approach, Obj. 4, p. 48, ans. c

The gender differences described by evolutionary theory
a. are universal to all humans.
b. are linked to specific genes.
c. can be explained in other, simpler ways.
d. must have a genetic basis because they have been maintained over many generations.

7. Summarize the traditional psychoanalytic approaches to gender, Obj. 5, p. 51, ans. b

Karen Horney differed from Freud in that
a. she felt that girls form a stronger superego than boys.
b. she felt men envied women's power to create new life.
c. she neglected the role of social and cultural forces in shaping personality.
d. she felt that boys experience castration anxiety.

8. Summarize the traditional psychoanalytic approaches to gender, Obj. 5, p. 52, ans. d

For Jung, the anima and animus
a. are present primarily in men.
b. are present primarily in women.
c. are present in a few men and a few women.
d. are present in all men and all women.

9. Summarize the feminist reinterpretations of psychoanalytic theory, Obj. 5, p. 53, ans. b

According to the feminist psychoanalytic theorist, Nancy Chodorow, to end the devaluation of women we must change society so that
a. children are exposed to men who value feminine behaviors.
b. women and men share parenting equally.
c. distinctions between women and men are no longer emphasized.
d. men acknowledge and allow expression of their anima.

10. Explain the core concepts of the social learning approach to gender, Obj. 6, p. 53, ans. d

Social learning theorists focus on the role of _____ in shaping gender-typed behavior.
a. power
b. psychosocial crises
c. schemas
d. models

11. Explain core concepts of the cognitive-developmental approach to gender, Obj. 6, p. 53, ans. c

The knowledge that a person remains a girl or boy regardless of their clothing, hair length, or the toys played with is called
a. gender-in-context.
b. gender schema.
c. gender constancy.
d. gender labeling.

12. Contrast the cognitive-developmental and social-cognitive approaches, Obj. 6, p. 54, ans. b

Both cognitive-developmental and social-cognitive theories see the child
a. as a passive learner who acquires gendered behavior through reinforcement and punishment.
b. as an active constructor of his or her gender identity.
c. as an anticipator of others' responses to his or her gendered behaviors.
d. as shaped by stages of gender identity formation.

13. Explain gender schema theory, Obj. 6, p. 55, ans. a

For the majority of white Americans, contact sports are seen as masculine and dancing is seen as feminine. This is an example of
a. gender schemas.
b. gender constancy.
c. gender labeling.
d. gender in context.

14. Explain gender schema theory, Obj. 6, p. 55, ans. b

Sidney is highly gender-schematic. How is this likely to affect his beliefs and behaviors?
a. It will have little effect on his beliefs and behaviors.
b. He will believe and behave as if women and men are very different from each other.
c. He will believe and behave as if women and men are very similar to each other.
d. He is likely to treat women as equals rather than as sex objects.

15. Describe the two general approaches taken by feminist gender researchers, Obj. 7, p. 55, ans. d

In the feminist standpoint approach,
a. a minimalist perspective is emphasized
b. the context of gender is emphasized.
c. gender schemas are emphasized.
d. the unique experiences of women are emphasized

16. Describe the two general approaches taken by feminist gender researchers, Obj. 7, p. 55, ans. c

The view that emphasizes similarities between genders and de-emphasizes the importance of any differences between them is called
a. maximalism.
b. gender-in-context theory.
c. minimalism.
d. feminist standpoint theory.

17. Describe the core concepts of the gender-in-context perspective, Obj. 8, p. 56, ans. a

Competitiveness, dependence, or domination is a product of an interaction, not a person according to the
a. gender-in-context approach.
b. essentialist perspective.
c. feminist standpoint approach.
d. maximalist perspective.

18. Describe the core concepts of the gender-in-context perspective, Obj. 8, p. 56, ans. a

When women are in superior status or in positions of power relative to other women or men,
a. they interact in ways that are more frequently observed in men.
c. they interact in ways that are stereotypically female.
d. their interactions vary according to the individual.
d. they interact in gender-appropriate ways.

19. Summarize the strengths and weaknesses of the psychological perspective, Obj. 9, p. 57 ans. b

Which theory does NOT have good scientific support?
a. Cognitive-developmental
b. Psychoanalytic
c. Gender schemas
d. Gender-in-context

20. Summarize the strengths and weaknesses of the psychological perspective, Obj. 9, p. 58, ans. d

Which theory is most sensitive to the social setting, status and cultural factors that affect gender?
a. Psychoanalytic
b. Social-cognitive
c. Cognitive-developmental
d. Gender-in-context

21. Summarize the strengths and weaknesses of the psychological perspective, Obj. 9, p. 58, ans. c

Which theory combines the strengths of social learning theory and cognitive-developmental theory?
a. Gender-in-context
b. Feminist standpoint
c. Gender schema
d. Social role

22. Contrast the traditional sociological perspective with the more feminist approach of social role theory, Obj. 10, p. 59, ans. b

Feminist sociologists reconstructed sociological gender theory by paying attention to the issue of
a. social construction.
b. power relationships.
c. regulation of sexuality.
d. group behavior.

23. Summarize the strengths and weaknesses of the sociological perspective, Obj. 11, p. 59, ans. d

Which of the following is NOT a weakness of the sociological perspective?
a. It does not allow for predicting individual behavior.
b. It cannot account for overlapping influences.
c. It can only point out correlations between gender related variables.
d. It does not offer insight into the functioning of societies.

24. Summarize the central concerns of the anthropological approach, Obj. 12, p. 60, ans. a

Contemporary anthropological studies demonstrate that
a. every human culture makes some distinction between women and men.
b. some human cultures do not make distinctions between women and men.
c. every human culture values men over women.
d. gender roles are fairly similar across cultures.

25. Summarize the core concepts of one Eastern approach to nature, Obj. 13, p. 61, ans. c

According to Chinese theory, everything in the universe is striving toward
a. power.
b. yin.
c. harmony.
d. yang.

Short-Answer Questions

26. Why do we need to study theories?

27. Name three qualities of a useful theory.

28. What is a criticism of evolutionary theory?

29. Why might the order of Erikson's adolescence (identity vs. role confusion) and early adulthood stages (intimacy vs. isolation) apply more to men than women?

30. Describe the stages of gender acquisition.

31. According to gender schema theory, what should happen if a society does not emphasize the distinctions between women and men?

32. Distinguish between a minimalist and a maximalist.

33. Explain the statement that "under the influence of certain cultural, interpersonal and situational factors, we 'do' gender," (p. 56).

34. Use social role theory to explain why women are more accurate in interpreting nonverbal communications.

35. Why is the anthropological perspective particularly useful in terms of understanding gender roles?

36. How is the concept of *yin* and *yang* unlike Western notions of opposites?

Essay Questions

37. Use the criteria for a good theory to evaluate one of the following theories: evolutionary theory, gender schema theory, gender-in context theory.

38. In what ways are cognitive-developmental theory, social cognitive theory, and gender schema theory alike? In what ways do they differ?

39. Which gender theory makes the most sense to you? Explain your choice.

Chapter 4
Gender and the Body

Learning Objectives

1. Summarize the findings, both conclusive and inconclusive, regarding sex differences in the hypothalamus and brain structures.

2. List and explain four issues surrounding the influence of gonadal hormones on human behavior, especially in the area of cognitive abilities.

3. Evaluate the stereotype that males excel in math, emphasizing the relevant cross-cultural findings.

4. Summarize the strengths and weaknesses of the research on sex/gender differences in verbal abilities and visuospatial abilities.

5. Explain how Carroll's (1998) study of group differences in fingerprint patterns illustrates the inherent weaknesses of sex difference research.

6. Explain why understanding the findings on gender differences in brain structure, hormonal influence, and cognitive abilities is important.

7. List the components of sex and gender development from chromosomal sex to the roles of the fully gendered adult.

8. List two types of sex chromosome disorders and three gonadal hormone disorders, and then summarize how these conditions influence various components of gender development.

9. Explain how intersexuality can help us understand the relationship between the body and gender, and then summarize the controversies regarding the response to intersexuality in current Western society.

10. Offer several cross-cultural examples of how the body, particularly the genitals, serve to mark and express gender in various societies.

Summary

◆ Prenatal gonadal hormones organize the hypothalamus and the pituitary gland. At puberty, these structures activate and regulate the menstrual and ovulatory cycles in women. In men, they maintain a relative steady state for androgen levels.

◆ Methodological weakness and replication difficulties permeate the research on human sex differences in neuroanatomical and neuroendocrine processes. The brain is plastic in response to postnatal experiences. Nevertheless, observed differences in some cognitive abilities are attributed to brain and hormonal factors.

◆ The concepts of mathematical, verbal, and visuospatial abilities are vague as well as broad.

Despite contradictory cross-cultural and multicultural evidence, the notion of male superiority in mathematics continues as a robust stereotype. A large proportion of males are more vulnerable to problems in verbal abilities. Inconsistent findings regarding visuospatial abilities appear strongly related to weaknesses in methodology and measures used in research.

♦ The markers and transitions from chromosomal sex to gendered adult behavior are usually smooth and congruent. The impact of sex chromosome abnormalities (Turner syndrome and supernumerary chromosomes) as well as discordant hormonal functioning (AIS, CAH, and 5a reductase deficiency) on gender development varies considerably.

♦ Genital appearance is the major determinant of sex categorization and gender assignment in the vast majority of societies. Intersexuality offers insights into the various components of sex and gender development. In Western culture sex and gender are considered dimorphic. This results in attempts to quickly "correct" the ambiguous genitalia of intersexuals through surgery. ISNA and similar organizations have been fairly successful in achieving reconsideration of the medical policies regarding genital surgery for intersexed infants. Intersexuals challenge us to rethink our ideas about sex, gender, and genitalia.

♦ Bodily modifications, particularly genital modifications, are powerful markers of gender and gender ideals across many cultures.

In-Class Activities

Lecture Suggestion:

Lecture: Stereotype Threat and Women's Math Performance

You may wish to include a discussion of stereotype threat in your presentation of gender and math abilities. As the text discusses, the stereotype of female inferiority in math is still very strong, despite evidence to the contrary. Stereotype threat occurs when a person who is a member of a group which has been negatively stereotyped, is in a situation where there is a risk of being judged by that stereotype. For example, when women (particularly women who are good at math) take a math test, they may worry that a failure will confirm the stereotype that women can't do math. When stereotype threat occurs, it may negatively impact on the person's performance. Studies by Quinn and Spencer (2001) and Spencer, Steele, and Quinn (1999) demonstrate the impact of stereotype threat on women's math performance.

In this research, it was found that college women did as well as college men on easy math tests, but when the math tests were more difficult, the women did less well than the men. Spencer et al. (1999) speculated that this was because on easy tests, anxiety due to stereotype threat is not likely to cause difficulties, but on challenging tests, this anxiety is likely to create additional pressures, which will interfere with performance. This hypothesis was tested by giving participants a difficult test and telling half of them that the test had demonstrated gender differences in the past (thus invoking stereotype threat), while telling the other half that the test had been shown to be gender-fair (thus removing stereotype threat). It was found that women performed as well as men when stereotype threat was removed. When stereotype threat was present, the women performed significantly worse than the men.
Quinn and Spencer (2001) discuss the significance of stereotype threat for women's math

achievement. They point out that while women have made gains in math performance, particularly in the classroom, they continue to underperform on some standardized tests and are less likely than men to go into math related majors or professions. This may be due to stereotype threat, which is less likely to be a factor in a classroom setting where they are working with familiar material in supportive conditions. When women must confront new or difficult material, especially in situations such as standardized tests where their abilities are being judged, stereotype threat is much more likely to negatively affect performance.

Research into stereotype threat demonstrates that gender differences in math performance may lie in the situation rather than in the individual's innate predisposition or internalized cultural messages. While it may be difficult to change a stereotype (which is certainly the case with women and math abilities!), this research indicates that finding ways to reduce stereotype threat may enable women to perform to their highest abilities. In these studies, telling women that the test was gender-fair was all that was required to improve their performance.

References:

Quinn, DM & Spencer, S.J. (2001). The interference of stereotype threat with women's generation of mathematical problem-solving strategies. *Journal of Social Issues, 57* (1), 55-71.

Spencer, S.J., Steele, CM and Quinn, DM Stereotype threat and women's math performance. *Journal of Experimental Social Psychology, 35,* 4-28.

Discussion/Activity Suggestions:

1. *Activity: Exploring Intersexuality, Circumcision, and Female Genital Mutilation Issues Online.* Students are usually fascinated by the material on intersexuality, and will probably be very interested in conducting some research on internet sites that deal with the issue from the perspective of intersexed people. There are many such websites, a particularly good one is sponsored by the Intersex Society of North America, www.isna.org. (You may also find this website useful in preparing for class. There is a nice handout you can download which contrasts traditional treatment paradigms with the newer, patient-centered model.)
   You may also wish to give students the opportunity to explore websites devoted to discussions of circumcision (a good website is www.nocirc.org) and female genital mutilation (try the World Health Organization's website, www.who.int/frh-whd/FGM/). Ask students to report on what they learned to the class.

2. *Zoom and Enlarge Activity: The Neuroscientist, the Feminist, and the Critical Thinker.* To help students follow the logic of this fairly complex discussion of fingerprint pattern research, divide them into small groups and ask them to make a list of suggestions for removing the biases from Hall and Kimura's study.

3. *Discussion:* Divide students into groups and ask them to discuss their early experiences with math. How did they feel about math when they were in school? Did their feelings change as they moved from elementary to middle school to high school? Did their parents and teachers encourage them in their math abilities? In what ways did they learn that boys were better at math than girls? Did their gender have an effect on their early experiences with math?

4. *Discussion:* Before you have presented the material on intersexed people, ask students "what makes a person a boy or a girl?" Ask them again after you have discussed this material.

Paper Assignment

Response Paper: Ask students to find a report of sex differences in cognitive ability in the popular media and write a response to it, using what they have learned about the problems with research on sex differences in cognitive abilities.

InfoTrac Exercises

1. Using the keyword search term **gender and math**, ask students to find an article which explores the issue of gender differences in math ability. Have them write a brief report on the article, including a discussion of what this article could add to the discussion of math and gender in the text.

2. Using the keyword search term **intersex**, ask students to find an article, which explores psychological, social or cultural aspects of intersexuality. What did they learn about the connection between body and gender from this article?

Test Bank for Chapter 4

Multiple Choice Questions

1. Summarize the findings regarding sex differences in the hypothalamus and brain structures, Obj. 1, p. 65, ans. b

Which of the following statements regarding hormones and the prenatal development of internal reproductive structures is true?
a. No hormonal action is necessary for the formation of male internal structures.
b. No hormonal action is necessary for the formation of female internal structures.
c. Hormonal action is necessary for the formation of both male and female internal structures.
d. Hormonal action is irrelevant to the formation of both male and female internal structures.

2. Summarize the findings regarding sex differences in the hypothalamus and brain structures, Obj. 1, p. 66, ans. c

Research on the SDN-POA of the hypothalamus has found that
a. there are twice as many cells in young adult women than there are in men.
b. there is no difference in cell count between heterosexual and homosexual men.
c. in men, large numbers of cells die after age 50, while among women, this occurs after age 70.
d. there are differences in cell count between lesbians and heterosexual women

3. Summarize the findings regarding sex differences in the hypothalamus and brain structures, Obj. 1, p. 66-67, ans. d

Critics of research on sex differences in the brain have pointed out that
a. brain tissue from cadavers is susceptible to postmortem changes
b. it has been difficult to replicate many of the studies that find differences
c. laboratory chemicals and research procedures can change brain tissue
d. all of the above

4. . Summarize the findings regarding sex differences in the hypothalamus and brain structures, Obj. 1, p. 67-68, ans. a

Researchers have suggested that structures in the brain may be related to
a. gender differences in the rates of neurological and psychiatric diseases.
b. greater incidence of transexualism among women than men.
c. gender differences in food preference.
d. higher incidence of immune disorders among women.

5. Explain issues surrounding the influence of gonadal hormones, especially in the area of cognitive abilities, Obj. 2, p. 68, ans. b

Sex differences in cognition
a. cannot be altered because they are created by the gonadal hormones.
b. are likely to be exaggerated due to the file drawer phenomenon.
c. are caused solely by the influence of the gonadal hormones.
d. have not received much interest from researchers.

6. Explain issues surrounding the influence of gonadal hormones, especially in the area of cognitive abilities, Obj. 2, pp. 68 and 70, ans. d

When researchers find sex differences they invariably mean "an average disparity," so that
a. that these differences don't apply to unusual people.
b. we can predict an individual's behavior pretty accurately.
c. there is generally little overlap between men and women.
d. there is almost always great overlap between men and women.

7. Evaluate the stereotype than males excel in math, Obj. 3, p. 73, ans. b

"Boys excel in math"
a. This statement is generally true for classroom tests and grades.
b. This statement is generally false in countries where women have equal opportunity.
c. This statement is generally false for standardized tests.
d. This statement is generally true for computation problems.

8. Evaluate the stereotype than males excel in math, Obj. 3, p. 73, ans. c

The stereotype of female math inferiority
a. is not generally held by classroom teachers.
b. is held by many mothers, but they do not apply it to their own daughters.
c. continues in North America, despite evidence to the contrary.
d. is generally supported by psychological research on gender and math abilities.

9. Summarize the strengths and weaknesses of research on sex/gender differences in verbal and visuospatial abilities, Obj. 4, p. 74, ans. a

Which is the most accurate conclusion regarding sex/gender differences in verbal abilities?
a. There are no consistent patterns of gender differences.
b. Women outperform men.
c. Men outperform women.
d. In childhood girls outperform boys, but this difference weakens in adulthood.

10. Summarize the strengths and weaknesses of research on sex/gender differences in verbal and visuospatial abilities, Obj. 4, p. 75, ans. c

Findings regarding sex/gender differences in visuospatial abilities are
a. insubstantial and inconsistent
b. substantial and consistent
c. substantial, but inconsistent
d. insubstantial, but consistent

11. Explain how Carroll's study of group differences in fingerprint patterns illustrates the inherent weaknesses of sex difference research, Obj. 5, p. 71, ans. d

According to Carroll's analysis of research, which shows the L> pattern of fingerprints is more common in women and gay men, we can conclude
a. Women and gay men are alike.
b. Fingerprints can be used to identity who is likely to become gay.
c. Sexual orientation could be biologically based.
d. This finding is likely an artifact of the methods and measurements used.

12. Explain why understanding the findings on gender differences in brain, hormone and cognitive abilities is important, Obj. 6, p. 75, ans. b

When researchers replaced the rod in the Rod and Frame test with a human figure and told participants it was a test of empathy, women outperformed men. What does this demonstrate?
a. Women have greater field dependence.
b. Contextual variables can affect performance.
c. Men are not empathetic.
d. There are sex differences in visuospatial skills.

13. Explain why understanding the findings on gender differences in brain, hormone and cognitive abilities is important, Obj. 6, p. 76, ans. b

In the last 20 years, gender differences in cognitive abilities
a. have remained about the same.
b. have gradually declined.
c. have markedly increased.
d. have reversed.

14. Explain why understanding the findings on gender differences in brain, hormone and cognitive abilities is important, Obj. 6, p. 76, ans. d

Which of the following statements on sex differences in cognitive abilities is true?
a. Most people do not believe there is such a difference.
b. Reports of such differences are generally ignored by the popular media.
c. Companies who recognize that there are such differences make better choices in hiring.
d. The belief that there are such differences affects women's participation in math and science.

15. List the components of sex and gender development, Obj. 7, p. 77, ans. b

Which of the following is a bodily component of sex and gender?
a. Reproductive functioning and fertility.
b. Gender-appropriate nonverbal behavior.
c. Sexual functioning.
d. Sexual orientation.

16. List sex chromosome and gonadal hormone disorders, and summarize how these conditions influence gender development, Obj. 8, p. 78 ans. c

Women with Turner syndrome
a. manifest a weak feminine identity.
b. are unusually tall.
c. have a strong interest in maternity.
d. show significant differences in brain anatomy.

17. List sex chromosome and gonadal hormone disorders, and summarize how these conditions influence gender development, Obj. 8, p. 80, ans. c

In _____syndrome, an individual is genetically male, but has typically female genitalia.
a. Turner's.
b. Klinefelter's.
c. androgen-insensitivity.
d. congenital adrenal hyperplasia.

18. List sex chromosome and gonadal hormone disorders, and summarize how these conditions influence gender development, Obj. 8, p. 80, ans. a

Which of the following is true of the gender development of individuals with CAH?
a. CAH boys are gentle, not violent or aggressive.
b. Most CAH girls are gynecophilic in their sexual orientation.
c. Both CAH boys and girls tend to have lower-than-average IQs and low academic achievement
d. CAH girls tend to display highly feminine activity levels, body postures and movements.

19. List sex chromosome and gonadal hormone disorders, and summarize how these conditions influence gender development, Obj. 8, p. 81, ans. d

Studies in the Dominican Republic of individuals with enzyme 5a reductase deficiency were considered important because
a. they showed how environmental influences can overcome biological influences
b. they demonstrated the existence of a third sex
c. they repudiated the belief that gender identity is congruent with hormonal activity
d. they contradicted the idea that gender assignment had to take place at a very young age

20. Explain how intersexuality can help us understand the relationship between the body and gender, Obj. 9, p. 82, ans. d

Which of the following is NOT an assumption of the *optimal* gender approach to the gender assignment of intersexed infants?
a. Gender arises solely from psychosocial rearing.
b. There is a critical period for gender identity development
c. The key component of gender is anatomy.
d. Experts should communicate to the parents that the infant's sex is ambiguous.

21. Explain how intersexuality can help us understand the relationship between the body and gender, Obj. 9, p. 85, ans. b

The John/Joan case demonstrates that
a. gender is completely a social creation.
b. biology does matter in gender development.
c. the optimal gender approach is the best way to think about gender assignment.
d. that gender assignment should not be based on the preferences of the intersexed individual.

22. Explain how intersexuality can help us understand the relationship between the body and gender, Obj. 9, p. 85, ans. b

According to members of the Intersex Society of North America, cosmetic genital surgery on intersexed infants and children
a. should continue in order to promote good psychosocial adjustment.
b. should be delayed until the intersexed person can give informed consent.
c. should be given only if the child's parents are fully informed about their condition.
d. should be delayed until medical experts can do a genetic, gonadal, and reproductive evaluation.

23. Explain how intersexuality can help us understand the relationship between the body and gender, Obj. 9, p. 87, ans. c

Transsexuals
a. have the same goals as intersexuals.
b. are born with atypical and incongruent genitals.
c. want their bodily sex and gender identity to match.
d. are primarily interested in maintaining reproductive and erotic capacities.

24. Offer several cross-cultural examples of how the genitals serve to mark and express gender, Obj. 10, p. 88, ans. d

Which of the following statements regarding circumcision is true?
a. It is always done during infancy.
b. It is no longer obligatory for Jewish and Moslem men.
c. Scientists agree that it is necessary for hygiene and disease prevention.
d. Some men's groups argue that it is a form of genital mutilation.

25. Offer several cross-cultural examples of how the genitals serve to mark and express gender, Obj. 10, p. 88, ans. c

For both girls and boys, genital modification is done for the same purpose:
a. to promote hygiene and prevent disease.
b. to improve sexual functioning.
c. to promote and ensure gender conformity.
d. all of the above.

Short-Answer Questions

26. Why do researchers focus on the *hypothalamus* in searching for sex differences in the brain?

27. Give an example of a sex difference, not related to reproductive abilities, which has been attributed to the effects of prenatal hormones. What is an alternative explanation for this difference?

28. What is the file drawer phenomenon?

29. What is a problem with using the SAT to test for gender differences in math or verbal abilities?

30. How might traditional measures of visuospatial abilities be gender biased?

31. Why is it hard to identify specific gender-related difficulties for people with extra sex chromosomes?

32. Why are studies of intersexuals problematic?

33. What does it mean to believe that genitals and gender are *dimorphic*?

34. What do intersexual activists want in terms of sex and gender identity?

35. Give three examples of ritual marking or altering of the genitals as a sign of gender or cultural membership.

Essay Questions

36. A friend of yours argues that women just aren't as good at math as men. How do you respond?

37. What common biases in gender difference research were revealed by Carroll's analysis of studies on group differences in fingerprint patterns?

38. Why is it important to understand the findings on gender differences in brain structure, hormonal influences, and cognitive abilities?

39. Why does the birth of an infant with ambiguous genitals create a psychosocial emergency in Western society?

39. Why can intersex people "be our best mentors and co-learners about sex and gender and about the meaning of the body in both of these" (p. 77)?

40. What does it mean to say that gender is mainly a social construction?

Chapter 5
Life Span Gender Development

Learning Objectives

1. Describe the important features of the gendered context within which infants and toddlers develop, emphasizing how mothering and fathering influence gender development.

2. Describe the important gender-related features of childhood development.

3. Explain the concept of gender intensification during adolescence and summarize the gender-related findings in four areas of development.

4. Explain three important issues in understanding adult gender development, and then summarize the findings regarding gender and the three major roles of adulthood.

5. Evaluate the evidence regarding the concept of a midlife gender transition.

6. Explain how culture and gender influence the caregiver role in later adulthood.

7. Explain how demographic trends have changed the realities of old age for the elderly and their families.

8. Summarize the important features of widowhood as a gendered role around the world.

9. Summarize the gender-related features at the end of life.

Summary

- Gender is a lifelong process. Infants and toddlers develop in the gendered environment provided by parents and society. Young children move from gender awareness to the complexities of full gender understanding and knowledge.

- Gender-differentiated work and play during childhood set the foundations for the gendered division of labor that characterizes traditional adulthood. Gender-segregated childhood peer groups have a powerful impact on later gender typing.

- Gender intensification marks the socially constructed period of life called *adolescence*. Gender similarities and differences in interpersonal relating, moral reasoning, body ideals, and self-esteem are some of the important gender themes of adolescence.

- Across all societies, the important tasks of adulthood involve the gendered roles of partnering, parenting, and making a living. All three areas are undergoing transformation in today's world. Contextual and situational factors offer the best explanations for inconsistencies regarding gender differences in behavior in these areas. Notions of midlife gender role crossover or convergence are not well supported, and they too seem related to contextual or situational variables.

- Later adulthood is characterized by caretaking for elderly parents, and this has been a heavily gendered role. The gendered meaning of retirement is undergoing change in the industrialized and postindustrial world.

♦ A growing segment of the world's population is made up of elderly women. Women's traditional gender role socialization better prepares them to cope with the physical decline and socioemotional losses associated with aging. Gender shapes the experiences of widowhood, grief, and even death.

In-Class Activities

Lecture Suggestion:

Lecture: Socialization into Powerlessness

One of the general themes of childhood gender socialization for girls described in the text is "acquisiton and acceptance of lower social status." In a multicultural research review Hilary Lips (2001), describes how a similar theme, "cultural preparedness for powerlessness", is transmitted to girls through socialization in childhood and adolescence.

Lips argues that girls receive strong and consistent messages of powerlessness—they learn that they are limited in their ability to exert control over a situation—from parents, teachers and peers. In particular, she focuses on powerlessness in two areas: mastery over tasks and influence over people. Some of the research she reviews is described below, in addition, much of the research cited in the text can also be tied into this theme.

Lips cites research which shows that parents emphasize emotions and elaborate more when talking to daughters than to sons, thus preparing daughters to be more sensitive to feelings and relationships, and to negotiate rather than demand. Parents emphasize mastery to sons when they give them toys that help develop instrumental and dominance-oriented behaviors, while girls are given toys that teach cooperation, accommodation, and support. Parents also encourage dependency in daughters by intervening more often in girls' play, controlling their behavior more often and being more directive than they are with sons. All of these socialization practices encourage girls to see themselves as less able to master challenges and influence people.

Teachers too, contribute to feelings of powerlessness in girls when they interact more often with boys, pay more attention to boys, provide boys with more feedback, and allow boys to talk in class more often. Boys learn from teacher feedback that failure means they just aren't trying hard enough. Girls on the other hand, are more likely to learn from teacher feedback that the task was easy for them because they are smart or that the teacher likes them.

Gender differences in peer interactions also prepare girls for powerlessness. Beginning in toddlerhood and increasing over the early years of school, boys are more likely to use direct modes of influence, such as orders or announcements. Girls are more likely to use indirect influence, stating requests as questions, or being polite about their requests. Boys' styles of play and friendship patterns give them practice in interactions that are competitive and dominance-oriented, while girls' interactions are more facilitative and supportive. Lips points out that these differences may make it more challenging for girls when they grow up and are in mixed-gender situations where they are interacting with men who have been socialized into a more dominant, competitive interaction style.

By adolescence Lips argues, girls are showing a pattern of lower self-esteem, self-confidence, and a readiness to believe that they are incapable of mastering certain situations. They have been trained into a "well-nurtured habit of silence and self-doubt" and "an abiding path of acquiescence," (p. 32).

References:

Lips, H. (2001). Female powerlessness: Still a case of "cultural preparedness'? In A.E. Hunter & C. Forden (eds.), *Readings in the Psychology of Gender: Exploring Our Similarities and Our Differences.* Boston: Allyn & Bacon.

Discussion/Activity Suggestions:

1. *Zoom and Enlarge Activity: Gender and Death.* Box 5.3 describes gender differences in mourning rituals. Ask students to discuss their own experiences of gender differences in the mourning and grieving process: Are men and women involved in different aspects of the viewing, the wake, the funeral, providing comfort to the bereaved, etc.? Do men and women express grief differently? Are there cultural differences in mourning practices within the class? Do gender differences hold across these cultural differences?

2. *Activity: A Gender Across the Life Span Panel.* With help from your students, invite a panel of males and females to class to discuss aging across the life span. Ideally, you should have a male and female from each of the following age groups: school age, adolescent, young adult, middle age, old age. Ask the panel to answer the following questions: What's good about being a boy (girl) or man (woman) at your age? What's hard about it? What's something you've learned about being a boy (girl) or man (woman) at your age? What's a piece of advice you have for a boy (girl) or man (woman) who's going to be your age? It seems to work most effectively if you line the panel up from youngest to oldest, ask a question, go down the line with their answers, and then ask the next question. You can also ask the class if they have any questions for the panel.

3. *Activity: Experiences with Gender Intensification.* Break students into groups of males and females. Ask the groups to discuss their own experiences with gender intensification. What examples do they have of gender intensification during their own adolescence? How did they feel about gender intensification? What examples do they have of times they violated gender roles in early adolescence? How did others respond to this violation? Did gender intensification affect their feelings of self-esteem? Have the groups report to the class. Did males and females experience gender intensification differently?

4. *Discussion:* Break students into small groups and ask them to discuss how their own parents (or other primary caregivers) influenced their understanding of gender roles. Have the groups report back to the class on what they learned in the discussion. Ask them what they would like to teach their own children about being a man or a woman.

Paper Assignment

Gender Biography: Ask students to interview a male or female over the age of 65 about the ways that their experiences with gender have changed over their lifetimes. Using what they have learned in class about life span gender development, ask students to develop a list of interview questions which will look at the person's experiences in childhood, adolescence, and adulthood. After the interview, students should compare the experiences of their interviewee to the descriptions of life span gender development discussed in class.

InfoTrac Exercise

Using the keyword search feature, look up articles on gender in a particular age group (keywords: **gender and infancy, gender and toddler, gender and childhood, gender and adolescence, gender and young adulthood, gender and middle age, gender and old age**.) Find an article that addresses one of the gender-related issues discussed in the text for that age group. What does this article add to the information in the text?

Test Bank for Chapter 5

Multiple Choice Questions

1. Describe the features of the gendered context within which infants and toddlers develop, Obj. 1, p. 93, ans. c

In a study of birth announcement cards in the United States,
a. Girl cards mentioned feelings of "happiness" more often.
b. Scenes of sleeping or lying down were more common in boy cards.
c. Announcements of a girl's birth used words such as "sweet" and "little" more often.
d. Boy cards occasionally featured scenes of physical activity or action.

2. Describe the features of the gendered context within which infants and toddlers develop, Obj. 1, p. 93, ans. d

Which society values female infants over males?
a. Bangladesh
b. 19th century rural America
c. China
d. Mukogodo of Kenya

3. Describe the features of the gendered context within which infants and toddlers develop, Obj. 1, p. 93, ans. b

What accounts for differences in mothers' developmental expectations between Japan and India?
a. Japan is a collectivist society.
b. There is a cojoint family structure in India.
c. Japanese mothers have more help with parenting tasks.
d. Indian society values self-sufficiency.

4. Describe the features of the gendered context within which infants and toddlers develop, Obj. 1, p. 94, ans. c

The impact of paid maternal employment on children's development
a. is generally negative.
b. is almost always positive.
c. is very complex.
d. is not significant.

5. Describe the features of the gendered context within which infants and toddlers develop, Obj. 1, p. 94, ans. b

Father involvement
a. makes sons more individualistic and strongly masculine.
b. increases empathy and sensitivity among sons.
c. is actually more important to sons' well-being than mother involvement.
d. makes sons more able to defend themselves from the more "feminine" aspects of the self.

6. Describe the features of the gendered context within which infants and toddlers develop, Obj. 1, p. 94, ans. c

In general, compared to mothers, fathers
a. are less likely to take care of their children in public settings.
b. do more teaching and less disciplining of toddlers.
c. do more playing.
d. take care of children while doing other tasks as well.

7. Describe the features of the gendered context within which infants and toddlers develop, Obj. 1, p. 95, ans. a

By what age do children possess gender scripts?
a. 3
b. 5
c. 7
d. 12

8. Describe the important gender-related features of childhood, Obj. 2, p. 95, ans. b

Which is NOT a gendered theme of childhood socialization for boys?
a. importance of peer group
b. flexibility of gender-typed behaviors
c. autonomy from adult supervision
d. rehearsal of occupational roles of adulthood

9. Describe the important gender-related features of childhood, Obj. 2, p. 95, ans. c

When it comes to play, girls
a. request gender-typed toys more often over time.
b. tend to enact more fantasy and occupational roles.
c. take pride in being able to do boy-typed activities.
d. prefer to play in larger groups.

10. Describe the important gender-related features of childhood, Obj. 2, p. 95, ans. b

Childhood gender segregation
a. begins at an earlier age for boys.
b. is universal.
c. allows for more behavioral flexibility.
d. all of the above.

11. Explain the concept of gender intensification during adolescence and summarize the findings in four areas of development, Obj. 3, p. 99, ans. c

In cross-cultural studies of adolescent relationships,
a. there is a great deal of variation in descriptions of intimacy
b. some cultures report greater levels of emotional connection in men
c. similarities within genders tend to override cultural differences
d. there were no overall patterns of gender differences.

12. Explain the concept of gender intensification during adolescence and summarize the findings in four areas of development, Obj. 3, p. 101, ans. d

Which of the following conclusions about gender differences in moral reasoning has the most support?
a. Women show higher levels of moral reasoning.
b. Men's moral reasoning is based on the principles of justice and individual rights.
c. Moral reasoning is gender-specific.
d. Men and women use both types of moral reasoning.

13. Explain the concept of gender intensification during adolescence and summarize the findings in four areas of development, Obj. 3, p. 101, ans. a

Which of the following statements about body image for adolescents in Western society is true?
a. Ideal body stereotypes divide along gender lines.
b. Adolescent males and females are similar in feeling dissatisfaction with their bodies.
c. In girls, a more positive body image was associated with lower masculinity scores.
d. Males prefer a large build and evaluate themselves on muscle size.

14. Explain three important issues in understanding adult gender development, and summarize findings regarding gender in adulthood, Obj. 4, p. 106, ans. d

A factor to consider in any discussion of adult gender issues is that
a. around the world, gender roles remain essentially unchanged.
b. the "gender in context" perspective is being replaced by the "gender stability" perspective.
c. there is a great deal of commonality across cultures in gender roles.
d. in virtually all its manifestations, gender is being reconstructed.

15. Explain three important issues in understanding adult gender development, and summarize findings regarding gender in adulthood, Obj. 4, p. 106, ans. d

In adult U.S. women, more egalitarian gender role attitudes are associated with
a. lower-status jobs.
b. stronger religious affiliation.
c. being foreign born
d. more years of education

16. Explain three important issues in understanding adult gender development, and summarize findings regarding gender in adulthood, Obj. 4, p. 107, ans. b

When women and men share the domestic and occupational spheres equally,
a. there continue to be differences in work values, attitudes and patterns.
b. they may still hold traditional gender role ideologies.
c. women usually struggle in their new managerial and professional roles.
d. all of the above.

17. Explain three important issues in understanding adult gender development, and summarize findings regarding gender in adulthood, Obj. 4, p. 108, ans. b

Which of the following statements regarding grandmothers is true?
a. 5 percent of African-American households are extended families that include a grandmother.
b. The highest level of involvement occurs among Mexican-Americans grandmothers.
c. Craft and community activities are more typical of grandmothers than grandfathers.
d. Paternal grandmothers are the most involved in childcare.

18. Evaluate the evidence regarding a midlife gender transition, Obj. 5, p. 107, ans. a

A midlife gender transition
a. is likely due to contextual rather than biological or intrapsychic causes.
b. continues to occur because young adults still experience the parental emergency.
c. is unlikely because a career is key to life satisfaction for both genders throughout adulthood.
d. is more common now than it was in the past because of more gender role flexibility.

19. Explain how culture and gender influence the caregiver role in later adulthood, Obj. 6, p. 109, ans. b

In families where there are sisters and brothers, who does most of the caretaking of elderly parents?
a. the oldest child, regardless of gender
b. the sisters
c. the brothers
d. it is evenly divided between sisters and brothers

20. Explain how demographic trends have changed old age, Obj. 7, p. 109, ans. c

Compared to men, women who retire
a. have fewer chronic health problems.
b. are less likely to live alone.
c. are more likely to be poor.
d. all of the above.

21. Explain how demographic trends have changed old age, Obj. 7, p. 111, ans. b

In a study of African-American people age 85 and over, it was found that
a. men received more help from distant family members.
b. women received more help from relatives and friends.
c. men received more help from fictive kin.
d. women received more help from immediate family members.

22. Explain how demographic trends have changed old age, Obj. 7, p. 111, ans. d

Who is better equipped to handle old age?
a. Men, because they maintain more extensive social networks.
b. Men, because they are more comfortable asking for help.
c. Women, because their friendships are based on shared activities.
d. Women, because they are more likely to receive support from multiple sources.

23. Summarize the important features of widowhood, Obj. 8, p. 111, ans. c

Which of the following statements regarding widowhood is true?
a. Widows lose status in developing nations, but not in industrialized nations.
b. Widows in all Islamic societies are entitled to only one eighth of their husband's wealth.
c. Globally, virtually all widows lose status.
d. Widows from the Hausa and Hokkien cultures have greater economic resources and status.

24. Summarize the gender-related features of the end of life, Obj. 9, p. 113, ans. c

Who is more vulnerable to stress-related illnesses after a bereavement?
a. Women, because they don't receive the emotional support they need from their husbands.
b. Women, because they are likely to spend too much take taking care of the needs of other people.
c. Men because they may be more reluctant to undertake the emotional work of grieving.
d. Men and women are equally vulnerable.

25. Summarize the gender-related features of the end of life, Obj. 9, p. 113, ans. a

Which of the following statements about gender-related differences in death is true?
a. Upper-class men outlive lower-class women.
b. Men are more likely to die after an extended period of chronic illness.
c. Women are less likely to experience the death of siblings and friends.
d. Women are more likely to die from suicide.

Short-Answer Questions

26. What are the three general trends that researchers have found in studies of the impact of increased involvement of fathers with their children?

27. Describe the sequence children follow in developing an understanding of gender.

28. What are three of the general gender themes of childhood gender socialization for girls?

29. Why are "tomboys" more acceptable than "sissies" to peers and parents?

30. Define *gender intensification*.

31. How were gender roles in the African-American community impacted by racism?

32. Is there a gender crossover in middle age? Explain.

33. What are three gender differences in care giving for elderly parents?

34. How will retirement be different for baby boom women than it is for women today?

35. What makes women better equipped to handle old age?

36. Describe two gender-related differences regarding death.

Essay questions

37. Are boys more aggressive than girls? What evidence supports your position?

38. Imagine that you are have just become the parent of either a baby boy or a baby girl. Given what you have learned about gender in infancy, childhood, and adolescence, what concerns will you have in raising your boy or girl? What will you do as a parent to address those concerns?

39. Why is the discussion of adult gender issues described as "somewhat like trying to capture wind in a box?"

40. Given what you have learned about gender in old age, what can you expect in your own old age? What can you do now to prepare for the ways that gender may impact you when you are old?

Chapter 6
Gender and Relationships

Learning Objectives

1. Briefly summarize the influence of gender in sibling relationships across the life span.

2. Summarize the important features of childhood and adolescent friendships for girls and boys, mentioning how these may be distinctive for those with same-sex orientation.

3. Contrast the popular stereotype with the relevant research findings regarding how men and women conduct their friendships, mentioning cross-sex friendships.

4. Explain how dating facilitates partner selection in individualistic societies, contrasting this with romantic relationships among sexual minorities.

5. Evaluate the claims of evolutionary psychologists regarding human universals in partner preferences.

6. Contrast the central features of the arranged marriage versus the love marriage.

7. Summarize the historical and current marital patterns among African Americans as an example of the love-based marriage.

8. Explain how the nuclear family came to be normative, and summarize the important features of Peplau's classic marriage classification scheme.

9. List and describe the forces that precipitated ongoing changes in gender-related marital and family roles.

10. Summarize the important features of the current issues surrounding the distribution of child care, housework, and parenting roles in the postindustrial family.

11. Summarize the findings regarding parenting roles and the distribution of household tasks among gay and lesbian families.

12. Summarize the gender-related issues surrounding divorce and repartnering.

Summary

♦ Relationships give our lives meaning and purpose. Sibling relationships last the longest, and gender influences sibling relationships all through the life span.

♦ Childhood friendships reinforce gender-typed behavior and preferences. Adolescent friendships are very important and influential. The masculine emphasis on sports facilitates the development of positional identities and activities-oriented relating among men. The behavioral norms for same-sex friends may be problematic for adolescents with a same-sex or bisexual orientation, especially boys. Friendship norms in other societies may vary considerably.

♦ Historically, men's friendships were more valued. Since the 1970s, women's friendships have become the idealized norm. Although there are gender differences in friendships, these moderate over time. Adult friendship patterns vary over the life span and among various special groups. Cross-sex friendships are becoming more common, but continue to be devalued.

♦ In more collectivist societies, arranged marriages prevail, but love marriages are becoming the global norm. Historical events shaped marital norms and patterns in the African-American community. Marital norms for the mainstream North American marriage evolved from the realities of the Industrial Revolution. Peplau (1987) described traditional, modern, and egalitarian marriages. Many factors precipitated the recent, massive, and ongoing changes in gender roles.

♦ In more individualistic societies, love and romance are the basis for marriage. Dating scripts are ritualized interactions based on gender. Cohabitation is increasingly common, and may precede or substitute for a traditional marriage. Gay men and lesbians also idealize romantic love as a basis for long-term relationships, but must construct these relationships without socially approved models. Recent research suggests that cross-cultural similarities in partner preferences are socioculturally, rather than biologically based.

♦ The postindustrial family is varied and complex in composition. Child care and housework remain the major arenas of gender-related contention in such families. The father role has undergone considerable scrutiny and reconstruction over the last two decades. The mother role has been synonymous with parenting, and this too is in the process of reconstruction. Lesbian and gay families are increasingly visible and offer an instructive alternative to gender-based division of family roles. Asian-American families are quite varied in terms of gender roles. Polygamous families demonstrate another form of family diversity.

♦ Divorce and repartnering are increasingly normative in postindustrial societies. One's gender influences the experience and meaning of divorce. The blended-family or step-family must renegotiate very complex family relationships without well-established norms or models.

In-Class Activities
Lecture Suggestion:

Lecture: Gender in Gay and Lesbian Relationships

As is described in the text, a good deal of behavior in relationships is guided by gender. For example, women do the majority of housework and childcare, and men take the initiative in dating. An article by Michelle Huston and Pepper Schwartz looks at how the work of relationships is divided when gender roles cannot be used as a guide—as in the case of gay and lesbian relationships.

As described in the text (p. 122), there are scripts for men and women which guide dating behavior. Masculine scripts are proactive while feminine scripts are reactive, and these complementary scripts make the dating process more predictable. Gay and lesbian dating partners on the other hand, do not have complementary scripts because both partners have been socialized into the appropriate script for their gender. As women, lesbians have learned to be reactive as so may have difficulty initiating dating and expressing romantic interest. Huston and Schwartz suggest that this may explain why so many lesbian relationships develop out of friendships. Gay men, on the other hand have been socialized to be proactive, so they are likely to be more at ease with initiating relationships, but are likely to have difficulty with being the one who is approached. They may not pursue relationships where they were the ones who were asked out.

Similar issues arise concerning sex. Most lesbians believe that there should be equal right of initiation and refusal of sex, but lesbian couples tend to fall into patterns where one member usually initiates and the other accepts or refuses. Contrary to traditional gender roles, the initiator role is often taken by the more emotionally expressive or "feminine" partner, probably because lesbian sex usually starts with displays of affection. The more powerful partner is usually the one who has the right of refusal. In gay male relationships, both partners have been trained into the initiator role. This can create problems when both think that they are surrendering their masculinity by not being the one to make the advance. Refusal of sexual advances can also be used as a power play, although it is likely not as satisfying a position since it is not a part of the traditional male role. Huston and Schwartz argue that if these issues are not resolved, sex for gay male couples can become a battle for control and assertion of masculinity.

The vast majority of lesbians and gay men want egalitarian relationships. Lesbians are more likely to succeed in this goal. Huston and Schwartz speculate that this could be due to the fact that lesbians are less likely to use money as a measure of worth and that due to sexism, they are more likely to have similar incomes. However, even when a large gap exists, money is not connected to power in lesbian relationships. Gay men do measure power in their relationships by income. The partner who earns more has more say in the relationship and does less housework. Unlike heterosexual couples, gay men and lesbians cannot use gender to divide housework (with the woman doing the bulk of it). Gay men are most likely to divide housework equally, with each man responsible for different types of chores. Lesbians are more likely to share all tasks equitably, either taking turns or doing chores together.

Huston and Schwartz conclude that while gay men and lesbians are freed from traditional gender-based ways of organizing relationships, this also requires that they take responsibility for creating their own solutions to these issues. In addition, same-sex couples must deal with the fact that because they have experienced similar gender role socialization, their relationship may lack certain skills that are usually provided by a partner of the other gender. Because gay and lesbian relationships must be created outside of traditional gender roles, they can be a model for heterosexuals who wish more egalitarian relationships. These relationships demonstrate that it is possible to overcome socialization and act outside of gender role training.

References:

Huston, M. & Schwartz, P. (1996). Gendered dynamics in the romantic relationships of lesbians and gay men. In J.T. Wood (Ed.), *Gendered Relationships,* (pp. 163-176). Mountain View, CA: Mayfield Publishing Company.

Discussion/Activity Suggestions:

1. *Zoom and Enlarge Discussion: The Postindustrial Father Role:* Box 6.5 provides a discussion of the controversies surrounding the role a father should play in a family. Ask students whey they stand on this issue. Are fathers (or mothers!) essential for children's well-being? Do fathers (or mothers) offer something unique to children? Are biologically-related parents better for children than step-parents? Do men require marriage in order to be committed to their children?

2. *Zoom and Enlarge Activity: The Postindustrial Father Role:* Ask your students to collect their own data on this issue by interviewing fathers on the following questions: What kinds of activities do you do with your children? What do you see as your role as a father? Is your role as a father different from a mother's role? What do you enjoy about being a father? You may want to assign students to interview a variety of fathers—at home fathers, dual earner fathers, fathers whose partners are at home mothers, divorced fathers who don't have custody, and stepfathers. Have student compare their research to the discussion offered in Box 6.5.

3. *Activity: Experiences with Cross-Sex Friendships.* Almost all college students in a study described in the text (p.120) report at least one cross-sex friendship. Ask your students to think about a particular cross-sex friendship they've experienced in high school or college, and write their answers to the following questions on an unsigned piece of paper: What is good about being friends with someone of the other gender? What is hard about it? What, if anything, have you learned about gender roles from this relationship? If students don't have a cross-sex friendship, ask them to discuss their reasons for not having such a friendship. When everyone has finished writing, collect the responses and break students into groups. Distribute the responses to the groups and ask them to summarize what the responses say about cross-sex friendship. Have each group report their findings to the class.

4. *Discussion:* Ask students to discuss their view of the ideal marriage/committed relationship. What role, if any, does gender play in their ideal relationship? How do their ideals compare to Peplau's three types of marriages? Do they think they will be able to achieve their ideal? Why or why not?

5. *Discussion:* Divide students into small groups. Ask each group to come up with a list of suggestions for creating egalitarian romantic relationships. The list should include both things that the students have tried and things they haven't tried. Have the groups share their suggestions with the class, and then ask them whether or not the suggestions are feasible. (This discussion would work well with the lecture material on gay and lesbian relationships.)

Paper Assignment

Analysis of Relationship Interventions: Ask students to research current intervention programs that are designed to improve marital or parental relationships (for example, Promise Keepers, parenting classes, premarital counseling, etc.). How is gender addressed in this intervention? What does the intervention assume about male and female roles in relationships? What role is gender seen as playing in relationship problems and success? Do you agree with the way this intervention treats gender? Why or why not?

InfoTrac Exercises

1. Using the keyword search, look up "gender and friendship," limiting the search to refereed publications. Find a study that addresses the issue of gender in friendship. Does the study report differences or similarities in friendship based on gender? Does the study support or refute the gender similarities and differences in friendship described on pp. 119 and 120 of the text?

2. Using the keyword search, look up "gender and housework." Find an article which provides you with an answer to the question "why is a discussion of housework included in a chapter on gender and relationships?"

Test Bank for Chapter 6

Multiple Choice Questions

1. Briefly summarize the influence of gender in sibling relationships, Obj. 1, p. 117, ans. a

In adulthood and old age, which sibling relationship tends to be the closest?
a. sister-sister
b brother-sister
c. brother-brother
d. both brother-brother and sister-sister

2. Summarize the important features of childhood and adolescent friendships for girls and boys, Obj. 2, p. 118, ans. c

Which of the following is NOT a theme of childhood friendships between boys?
a. loyalty
b. helping
c. closeness
d. awareness of each other's needs

3. Summarize the important features of childhood and adolescent friendships for girls and boys, Obj. 2, p. 118, ans. c

In adolescence,
a. girls' friendships focus mainly on activities.
b. boys' friendships focus mainly on verbal interaction.
c. girls' friendships focus mainly on verbal interaction and shared activities.
d. boys' friendships focus mainly on verbal interaction and shared activities.

4. Contrast the popular stereotype with the relevant research on friendship for men and women, Obj. 3, p. 119, ans. d

Historically,
a. male friendship was situated in the private rather than public sphere.
b. men were portrayed as unable to commit to each other.
c. feminine friendship was a moral and civic virtue.
d. women were seen as incapable of true friendship.

5.   Contrast the popular stereotype with the relevant research on friendship for men and women, Obj. 3, p. 119, ans. a

Men prefer friendships which
a. meet the ideals of intimacy and interpersonal sensitivity.
b. emphasize reciprocity.
c. are "face to face."
d. are complex and holistic.

6. Contrast the popular stereotype with the relevant research on friendship for men and women, Obj. 3, p. 120, ans. d

Lesbian friendships are distinctive because
a. they are more likely to cross language and ethnic boundaries.
b. there is a frequent mix of friendship and kin relationships.
c. "side by side" relationships are more frequent.
d. deep friendships are often maintained with former romantic partners.

7. Contrast the popular stereotype with the relevant research on friendship for men and women, Obj. 3, p. 120, ans. c

Cross-sex friendships
a. are more emotionally satisfying for women than men.
b. are not common among undergraduates.
c. give men relief from the rivalry of male friendships.
d. are highly valued in society.

8. Explain how dating facilitates partner selection, Obj. 4, p. 122, ans. b

Dating scripts for mainly white undergraduates in the United States
a. were not gender-typed
b. were proactive for males
c. were expressive for females
d. were not consciously practiced

9. Explain how dating facilitates partner selection, Obj. 4, p. 123, ans. b

When it comes to romantic love,
a. men and women look for different qualities in their mates.
b. feminine-typed men are better partners than traditionally masculine men.
c. women are generally more idealistic and romantic about love.
d. androgynous men and women are not good romantic partners.

10. Contrast romantic relationships among sexual minorities, Obj. 4, p. 124, ans. d

For lesbian couples,
a. sex generally occurs on the first date.
b. traditional gender role prescriptions guide romantic behavior.
c. friendship rather than romantic love is seen as the basis for long-term partnering.
d. living together is more likely to have a marital meaning.

11. Evaluate claims of evolutionary psychologists regarding partner preferences, Obj. 5, p. 124, ans. c

Which of the following is an evolution-based explanation for cross-cultural similarities in mate selection?
a. an attractive partner gains a man status among other men.
b. in societies with little educational freedom for women, women prefer wealthy men.
c. men seek features that are associated with reproductive success.
d. none of these are evolution-based explanations.

12. Contrast the central features of the arranged marriage versus the love marriage, Obj. 6, p. 124, ans. c

In rural north India where the majority of marriages are arranged, girls
a. are highly passive and accepting of their low status in their husband's family.
b. are formally educated so that they can run a large household more effectively.
c. are socialized to be demure and undemanding so they can live with their in-laws.
d. are under the control and tutelage of their father-in-law.

13. Contrast the central features of the arranged marriage versus the love marriage, Obj. 6, p. 124, ans. d

In contrast to love marriages, arranged marriages in China
a. are now the exception rather than the rule.
b. seem to result in greater marital satisfaction for women.
c. prescribe gender-based social asymmetry.
d. include a daughter-in-law role that takes precedence over that of a wife.

14. Summarize marital patterns among African Americans, Obj. 7, p. 125, ans. a

Historically, African-American marriages
a. have been based almost solely on attraction and affection.
b. generally took place without the slaveholder's knowledge.
c. were based on an economic hierarchy where the wife had more power.
d. during slavery formed the basis for defining who was "family."

15. Summarize marital patterns among African Americans, Obj. 7, p. 125, ans. b

Today, most black marriages
a. involve female domination.
b. involve mutual decision making.
c. involve economic disparity.
d. involve male passivity.

16. Summarize marital patterns among African Americans, Obj. 7, p. 126, ans. c

Why do African-Americans marry less than other ethnic groups in the United States?
a. Marriage is not highly valued.
b. Cohabitation is seen as more practical.
c. There is a lack of available men.
d. All of the above.

17. Explain how the nuclear family came to be normative, Obj. 8, p. 128, ans. b

Which of the following historical events was responsible for creating the nuclear family?
a. World War II
b. Industrialization
c. Urbanization
d. World War I

18. Explain how the nuclear family came to be normative, Obj. 8, p. 128, ans. a

The "cult of true womanhood"
a. celebrated domesticity, morality, and maternity.
b. encouraged devotion to work and material acquisition.
c. defined females as helpless, dependent, and fragile.
d. saw women's contributions to society as more valuable than men's.

19. Summarize Peplau's marriage classification scheme, Obj. 8, p. 128, ans. c

The husband in the modern marriage
a. shares equal power with his wife.
b. sees his wife's employment as of primary importance.
c. helps out with the child care.
d. all of the above

20. Summarize Peplau's marriage classification scheme, Obj. 8, p. 129, ans. d

When it comes to marital conflict, wives_____ while husbands_____.
a. avoid difficult discussions, confront.
b. defer in public, confront in public.
c. deny problems, withdraw.
d. bring up problems, avoid.

21. Describe the forces that precipitated ongoing change in marital and family roles, Obj. 9, p. 129, ans. a

Which of the following is NOT one of the forces for gender role change?
a. decreasing industrialization and urbanization
b. development of oral contraceptives
c. jobs requiring more education and training
d. ideal of companionate marriage

22. Summarize current issues surrounding child care, housework, and parenting, Obj. 10, p. 131, ans. b

When it comes to child care,
a. most husbands share tasks equally if their wives are employed.
b. fathers merely assist and participate rather than share in the responsibilities.
c. all mothers are eager to share their role with their spouse.
d. a father's role now generally goes beyond recreational activities.

23. Summarize current issues surrounding child care, housework, and parenting, Obj. 10, p. 131, ans. d

An involved and loving father
a. predicts appropriate gender role development in children.
b. causes children to be higher achieving.
c. lowers the risk of drug abuse for children.
d. facilitates a child's sense of security and belonging.

24. Summarize current issues surrounding child care, housework, and parenting, Obj. 10, p. 134, ans. c

Which of the following statements regarding the mother role is FALSE?
a. The sheer physical work of mothering is often underestimated and unexpected.
b. Many mothers exist with a constant and special awareness of their children.
c. Mothering means similar things among various cultural groups.
d. The mother role offers a good illustration of a gender ideal.

25. Summarize the findings regarding gay and lesbian families, Obj. 11, p. 135, ans. a

Lesbian couples,
a. divide housework on the basis of skill and interest.
b. typically demonstrate the same parenting awareness as heterosexual couples.
c. have a lower relationship quality than heterosexual couples.
d. value caretaking, nurturance and family connections less than heterosexual women.

26. Summarize the findings regarding gay and lesbian families, Obj. 11, p. 136, ans. b

Compared to heterosexual fathers, gay fathers
a. are more likely to emphasize play over nurturing.
b. are less likely to sexually abuse children.
c. are more likely to have children with low levels of autonomy.
d. all of the above.

27. Summarize the gender-related issues surrounding divorce and repartnering, Obj. 12, p. 136, ans. a

In describing reasons for divorce,
a. women complain of the lack of communication and shared interests.
b. women complain of immaturity and irresponsibility.
c. men complain of lack of affection.
d. men complain about inadequate quality of sex.

28. Summarize the gender-related issues surrounding divorce and repartnering, Obj. 12, p. 138, ans. d

When looking at the "patterns and peaks" of distress in divorce,
a. men find the period before deciding to end the marriage most difficult.
b. women feel the loss more strongly afterward.
c. women are more likely to harbor fantasies of reconciliation.
d. men are much less accepting of the end of their marriages.

Short-Answer Questions

29. What is one way that sibling gender is a factor in family relationships?

30. What role do organized sports play in developing mainstream masculinity?

31. What are the issues that confront gay and lesbian adolescents as they become aware of erotic attractions in the context of friendship?

32. What similarities do men and women share in dating preferences?

33. Respond to the evolution-based explanation for cross-cultural similarities in mate selection.

34. What is the doctrine of "separate spheres?"

35. Describe one of the forces for social change. What impact did it have on gender roles?

36. Why might it be difficult for men to act out the reconstructed father role?

37. What does it mean to say that "mothering exists in a situational and cultural context," (p. 135)?

38. What is the impact of having gay or lesbian parents on children?

39. What is a factor that helps explain the high rate of divorce in postindustrial society?

Essay questions

40. Is friendship between women different than friendship between men? What research supports your answer?

41. Explain the statement that "mainstream white notions of female subordination and male domination have never applied to African-American families," (p. 125).

42. Contrast the traditional, modern, and egalitarian marriage types.

43. Should fathers and mothers play different roles in their children's lives? Justify your answer using what you have learned about the father role and the mother role.

44. Describe how divorce affects women differently than men.

Chapter 7
Gender as Social Performance

Learning Objectives

1. List and describe seven essential qualities by which women and men have been traditionally differentiated.

2. Summarize the central features of the agentic/instrumental and communal/expressive styles.

3. List the three components of emotion, and summarize the evidence supporting the notion that emotions are, in part, social constructions.

4. Explain the relationship between traditional femininity and the expression of positive emotions and the relationship between masculinity and lack of emotionality.

5. Offer a brief critique of the essentialist perspective on gender and emotions, and contrast this with the insights offered by the gender-in-context perspective.

6. Summarize the gender-related factors involved in the nonverbal channels of touch and facial display.

7. Evaluate the current stereotype regarding gender differences in communication, and then summarize the findings regarding contextual factors in gender-typed communication.

8. Explain why eliminating sexist language is desirable, and offer some examples of nonsexist terminology.

9. Summarize the current findings regarding the ostensible gender differences in seven important personality-related social behaviors, emphasizing the cultural and contextual factors that influence these behaviors.

10. Summarize the cross-cultural findings regarding how sociocultural change influences the performance of gender.

Summary

♦ Over the centuries, scholars have attempted to describe or capture the essential differences between men and women in a variety of ways. Psychologists and sociologists use the terms *masculinity* and *femininity* to refer to the degree to which men and women have incorporated their society's gender ideals into their identity.

♦ The terms *communal/expressive* and *agentic/instrumental* have been used to summarize the core features of mainstream Western ideals for masculinity and femininity.

♦ A gender-biased notion of emotional expressiveness is a central feature of the feminine stereotype in mainstream culture. Contextual and situational variables predict variations in emotional expressiveness more reliably than does gender.

♦ Ostensible gender differences in touch and smiling also vary according to cultural and situational norms.

♦ Popular writings about strong gender differences in verbal communication reflect white, middle-class norms and expectations. Contextual and situational factors, especially status, exert strong influences on communication differences.

♦ The conversations of women and men are quite similar in content. Sexist language has undesirable effects on individuals, especially girls and women.

♦ The findings related to powerful stereotypes regarding gender differences in several personality traits and their associated social behaviors merit critical evaluation. These include achievement, aggression, assertiveness, conformity, empathy, helping behavior, and leadership.

♦ Cross-cultural research conducted in societies undergoing rapid sociocultural change in the direction of greater gender equality reveal a pattern of declining gender differences. These findings mirror the changes in our own society.

In-Class Activities

Lecture Suggestion:

Lecture: Gender, Leadership and Context

The text addresses the issue of gendered leadership fairly briefly, and you may wish to expand on this topic. A good source of material for a lecture on leadership is a recent issue (Winter 2001) of the *Journal of Social Issues, 57* (4), on the topic of "Gender, Hierarchy and Leadership." One of the articles from this volume by Janice Yoder, addresses strategies for making leadership work more effectively for women.

Yoder argues that there are two central issues to consider in developing strategies to help women be more effective leaders. First, it is necessary to understand that the way women act as leaders is intertwined with their realization that as women, they must contend with feminine stereotypes. Second, it is important to recognize that leadership occurs within a gendered social context. This context will affect which leadership tactics will be successful for women. Leadership strategies that work well for men may not be effective for women, and what is effective for women will depend upon the context of the leadership.

An highly uncongenial atmosphere for women leaders is one which is male dominated (especially if the woman is alone or a token); where the task is stereotypically masculine; the only rewarded goal is task completion; and hierarchy and power differences are emphasized over egalitarianism. Under these circumstances, leadership behaviors that are effective or neutral for men are more likely to work against women. Domination tactics that enhance the status of a male leader (e.g., sitting at the head of the table, assertiveness, being dominant, autocratic, directive, and agentic) create an unfavorable impression for female leaders. These tactics, *under uncongenial circumstances*, make women more disliked, less influential and more ineffective as leaders.

Yoder outlines three types of strategies that can be employed to make women more effective leaders in an uncongenial atmosphere: individual, organizational, and contextual.

Individual strategies: Since status enhancement strategies work against female leaders, women need to assert authority by breaking down status differences rather than by using their higher status to command and control. Talking and listening to subordinates, avoiding dominant speech acts, using humor during tense moments, and being respectful of others, can enable women to lead effectively in an uncongenial atmosphere. Women can also break down status differences by using motivation strategies that are group-oriented rather than self-oriented. In addition, women are more likely to be able to introduce innovations to a group if they are initially conforming to group norms and become solidly entrenched in a group before they attempt to make changes. A final strategy is to be exceptionally competent—research demonstrates that women who are highly competent exert more influence—but as Yoder, points out, this solution is fundamentally unfair.

Organizational supports: Because it is unfair to make women leaders shoulder all of the responsibility for their success in an uncongenial atmosphere, Yoder argues that organizations should provide women leaders with the support they need to be effective. Research shows that having the resources necessary to reward others, enhances a leader's effectiveness. Organizations can take steps to ensure women leaders have the resources they need to promote the well-being of their subordinates. In addition, organizations can legitimize a women leader, by providing her with necessary training and making the work group aware of her expertise. Although legitimization benefits both sexes, it is especially important for women who are less likely to be assumed to be competent if the task is stereotypically masculine.

Context changes: Leadership can also be enhanced by changing the context from uncongenial to congenial. One way to do this is to add women to the group. A group that is from 35% to 40% women is one where the context becomes truly congenial. Other contextual changes can include making tasks more socially complex, making groups longer term, and including tasks that require skills more commonly possessed by women than men.

References:

Yoder, J.D. (2001). Making leadership work more effectively for women. *Journal of Social Issues, 57* (4), 815-828.

Discussion/Activity Suggestions:

1. *Zoom and Enlarge Activity: Communicating Mainstream Masculinity and Femininity:* Box 7.3 provides a list of "mainstream, Western, middle-class, gender-related behavioral prescriptions." Break students into groups and ask them to generate a list of circumstances in which they have felt pressured to act out these prescriptions. Be sure to point out that men and women may experience both femininity and masculinity prescriptions. When you reconvene as a class, ask the groups to report on what they found in the exercise. What forces made them feel the need to act out a gender prescription? How did they feel when they complied? Is it generally a good decision to comply with gender prescriptions?

2. *ABCs of Gender Discussion: Dealing with Sexist Language:* Ask students to make suggestions for nonsexist alternatives to the list of words provided in Box. 7.2. Some of these words have already been fairly widely replaced (e.g., police officer for policeman), while others have not (workman's compensation). Ask students to describe what difficulties they see (if any) to making further changes in language. Why are people resistant to changing language? Although it is not on the list, you may also wish to ask students for suggestions on replacing the generic use of "he".

3. *Activity: Gender and Status Differences in Communication:.* Begin by asking students to generate a list of the ways that status differences are communicated in the classroom. In what ways do the students communicate their low status in the classroom? Are these similar to the stereotypes of feminine behavior? In what ways do teachers convey their high status? Are these similar to the stereotypes of masculine behavior? Next, ask students to think of a situation where they are a high status person. Have them generate a list of the ways they communicate their high status in that situation. Compare the high status behaviors in the classroom and elsewhere. Are they similar to masculine stereotypes? Do the men and women in the class act similarly when they are in a high status position? Do individuals display consistent communication behavior across high and low status situations, or does their behavior vary according to the situation? This exercise should help make the point that gender differences may in fact be more a function of status differences.

Paper Assignment

Research Review: On p. 160 in the text, Galliano argues that there has been "a conceptual change within the study of gender," and then she describes more specifically what this change has been. Ask students to conduct a research review to see if Galliano's claim is correct. They should choose one of the areas discussed in this chapter (e.g., emotions, language, aggression) and find articles on this topic from each of the following decades: the 70's, 80's, 90's and the present. In their review they should describe the approach researchers took in addressing gender differences. How has the understanding of gender differences in this area changed over the years? Are there aspects of understanding that have remained the same? Do the changes follow the pattern Galliano describes?

InfoTrac Exercises

1. Using the keyword search term **sexist language**, find an article that makes recommendations for changing language to eliminate sexism. What suggestions are made? How feasible are these suggestions? How do you think people will respond to these suggestions? Should these recommendations be implemented? Why or why not?

2. Using the keyword search term **agentic and communal**, find an article that discusses gender differences using this distinction. What findings regarding this gender difference are reported? Is this difference seen as relatively stable or a result of situational influences?

Test Bank for Chapter 7

Multiple Choice Questions

1. List and describe seven essential qualities by which women and men have been traditionally differentiated, Obj. 1, p. 142, ans. c

Which of the following is NOT one of the essential qualities that has been attributed to women?
a. "deficient and inadequate"
b "sameness and connectedness"
c. "higher"
d. "emotional"

2. Summarize the central features of the agentic/instrumental and communal/expressive styles, Obj. 2, p. 142, ans. c

The terms_____have been used to describe the core features of the masculine style.
a. rational/achievement
b. communal/expressive
c. agentic/instrumental
d. separateness/developed

3. Summarize the central features of the agentic/instrumental and communal/expressive styles, Obj. 2, p. 143, ans. a

In the communal/expressive style, the focus is on
a. harmony, cooperation and support.
b. status, dominance and asymmetry.
c. instrumental rewards and connection.
d. self-preservation and competency.

4. Summarize the central features of the agentic/instrumental and communal/expressive styles, Obj. 2, p. 143, ans. d

The agentic/instrumental style is associated with
a. sharing with others.
b. being warm.
c. enticing others.
d. being resourceful.

5. List the three components of emotion, Obj. 3, p. 144, ans. b

An expressive component of happiness is
a. saying "I feel happy."
b. smiling.
c. a feeling of excitement in your stomach.
d. an inner feeling of joy.

6. Summarize the evidence supporting the notion that emotions are social constructions, Obj. 3, p. 144, ans. d

Which of the following statements about culture and emotion is true?
a. Societies vary in terms of display rules for emotion.
b. Culture guides which feelings will be experienced in a given situation.
c. All human beings experience the same emotions and express them in the same way.
d. All of the above.

7. Explain relationship between femininity, masculinity and emotions, Obj. 4, p. 145, ans. b

Which of the following is NOT part of the gender stereotypes regarding emotionality?
a. Women have greater knowledge about emotions.
b. It is OK for men to display emotions if they are positive.
c. Emotional expressiveness is related to relationality and communality.
d. Emotionality is antithetical to rationality.

8. Critique the essentialist perspective on gender and emotions, Obj. 5, p. 145, ans. b

Emotionality
a. is a stable personality trait.
b. is intertwined with the feminine stereotype.
c. has been proven to be a source of gender differences.
d. is consistent across cultures.

9. Contrast the essentialist perspective on emotions with the gender-in-context perspective, Obj. 5, p. 146, ans. a

Current research on emotion suggests that
a. women and men are probably equivalent in their subjective experience of emotion.
b. men have a stronger subjective experience of emotion than women.
c. women have a stronger subjective experience of emotion than men.
d. only in childhood do males and females differ in their subjective experience of emotion.

10. Contrast the essentialist perspective on emotions with the gender-in-context perspective, Obj. 5, p. 146, ans. c

According to the gender-in-context perspective, who is most likely to express anger?
a. females
b. males
c. it depends upon the circumstances
d. it depends upon testosterone levels

11. Summarize the gender-related factors in nonverbal display, Obj. 6, p. 147, ans. c

Which of the following is NOT a primary factor in determining touching behavior?
a. status
b. social setting
c. gender
d. culture

12. Summarize the gender-related factors in nonverbal display, Obj. 6, p. 147, ans. d

What can we conclude from research on smiling?
a. Across all cultures, women are expected to smile more than men.
b. Politicians who smile are regarded more positively, particularly if they are men.
c. Smiling is primarily guided by internal emotional states.
d. The meaning of a smile varies across cultures.

13. Evaluate the current stereotype regarding gender differences in communication, Obj. 7, p. 148, ans. b

According to Deborah Tannen, women primarily use conversations to
a. achieve status.
b. reach consensus.
c. avoid intimacy.
d. maintain the upper hand.

14. Evaluate the current stereotype regarding gender differences in communication, Obj. 7, p. 149, ans. d

The use of tag questions, hedges, and qualifiers
a. does not vary by age.
b. is more common among women across all languages.
c. is not influenced by the gender composition of the group.
d. depends on the nature of the conversation.

15. Evaluate the current stereotype regarding gender differences in communication, Obj. 7, p. 151, ans. b

Gender-stereotypic communication patterns
a. are greater in groups where people know each other.
b. are more likely when members of one gender are in the minority.
c. are more common in dyads than in larger groups.
d. are less likely to emerge in socially ambiguous situations.

16. Evaluate the current stereotype regarding gender differences in communication, Obj. 7, p. 151, ans. c

When is a woman LEAST likely to conform to gender stereotypic communication behavior?
a. when she is in a powerless position
b. when she is flirting with a man
c. during interpersonal conflicts
d. during interactions with strangers

17. Evaluate the current stereotype regarding gender differences in communication, Obj. 7, p. 151, ans. c

Most contemporary researchers have concluded that
a. most gender differences in communication occur across situations and contexts.
b. gender is irrelevant to understanding communication patterns.
c. gender factors in communication are situationally variable.
d. gender is the primary factor in communication behavior.

18. Evaluate the current stereotype regarding gender differences in communication, Obj. 7, p. 152, ans. d

In a study of same-sex dyads, the most common topics of conversation were_____for women and _____for men.
a. men, sports
b. women, work
c. personal problems, leisure activities
d. there were no gender differences in the topics

19. Explain why eliminating sexist language is desirable, Obj. 8, p. 153, ans. a

When girls read vocational material that uses the generic masculine,
a. their self-confidence in their ability to participate in that profession is lowered.
b. they are more likely to imagine themselves experiencing success in that profession.
c. it has no impact on their ability to envision themselves doing that profession.
d. it encourages them to see themselves as able to participate in a "masculine" profession.

20. Explain why eliminating sexist language is desirable, Obj. 8, p. 153, ans. a

Which of the following is an example of nonsexist terminology?
a. police officer
b. waiter
c. mankind
d. airline steward

21. Summarize findings regarding gender differences in personality-related social behaviors, Obj. 9, p. 155, ans. b

Which parents in the United States are likely to have higher educational aspirations for their daughters than their sons?
a. middle-class mothers.
b. working-class minority parents.
c. poor Chicano families.
d. all of the above.

22. Summarize findings regarding gender differences in personality-related social behaviors, Obj. 9, p. 156, ans. c

Which of the following statements regarding physical aggression is true?
a. In some cultures, women are more physically aggressive than men.
b. Gender is not a significant factor in physical aggression.
c. Across cultures, men are more physically aggressive than women.
d. It is rare for women to use physical aggression.

23. Summarize findings regarding gender differences in personality-related social behaviors, Obj. 9, p. 156, ans. b

Researchers have found that women tend to view aggression as a way to_____, while men tend to view it as a way to _____.
a. achieve goals, deal with feelings when out of control
b. express feelings, gain control
c. gain control, achieve goals
d. deal with feelings when out of control, express feelings

24. Summarize findings regarding gender differences in personality-related social behaviors, Obj. 9, p. 157, ans. a

Which of the following statements most accurately portrays the relationship between testosterone and aggression?
a. Experience and resources seem to modulate any effects of testosterone.
b. Testosterone levels cause certain aggressive behaviors.
c. A person is likely to behave aggressively when their testosterone level is high.
d. In women, higher testosterone levels are associated with aggressive behavior.

25. Summarize findings regarding gender differences in personality-related social behaviors, Obj. 9, p. 157, ans. b

Research on assertiveness has demonstrated that
a. women are less assertive than men.
b. men do not respond favorably to assertive women.
c. gender role identification does not affect assertiveness.
d. all of the above.

26. Summarize findings regarding gender differences in personality-related social behaviors, Obj. 9, p. 159, ans. a

In a multicultural study of dominance and leadership, researchers found that
a. the higher the cultural status of women, the more women expressed dominance and leadership.
b. there were no gender differences in dominance and leadership across cultures.
c. men consistently expressed more dominance and leadership across cultures.
d. in the egalitarian culture, women expressed more dominance and leadership than men.

27. Summarize the cross-cultural findings regarding the performance of gender, Obj. 10, p. 160, ans. b

As sociocultural changes create greater gender equality
a. gender differences have remained stable.
b. there has been a decline in gender differences.
c. there has been a slight increase in gender differences.
d. gender differences have increased in some cultures and declined in others.

Short-Answer Questions

28. Describe two of the core essences that have been used to distinguish men and women.

29. What evidence supports the idea that emotions are socially constructed?

30. How might demand characteristics play a role in producing gender differences in emotion?

31. How does gender role identification affect the expression of anger?

32. Do women touch more than men? Explain your answer.

33. Name three of the contextual factors that influence gender differences in communication.

34. Why should we change sexist language?

35. What are the methodological flaws in research on gender differences in aggression?

36. What factors influence helping by men and women?

37. Why have gender differences declined as the status of women has risen in societies?

Essay questions

38. A friend you yours argues that "women are more emotional than men." How do you respond to this claim?

39. Use the interactionist model of gender-related behavior to explain why a woman who is usually quite outspoken when she is with her female friends, becomes quiet and tentative when she is with a group of male strangers.

40. Does testosterone cause aggression? Explain.

41. What does this chapter have to say about gender differences?

Chapter 8
Gender and Sexuality

Learning Objectives

1. Summarize the gendered aspects of sexual development, mentioning adolescent sexual scripts and the significance of first intercourse.

2. Define *sexual orientation*, and contrast the social meaning of same-sex sexual behavior in the West with its meaning in other societies.

3. Summarize the current findings regarding the origins of sexual orientation.

4. Summarize Masters and Johnson's sexual response model, emphasizing gender similarities and differences, and mentioning how culture influences sexual response.

5. List and explain several gender-related beliefs that influence contemporary sexual attitudes and behavior in Western society.

6. Summarize the gender similarities and differences in autoerotic behavior, and then describe the central features of contemporary Western feminine and masculine eroticism.

7. Explain the significance of fertility and infertility in adult social identity, and then explain how gender and culture influence patterns of contraceptive use and abortion.

8. Describe the gender-related aspects of selected categories of sexual dysfunction.

9. Summarize the gender-related features of two types of commercialized sex.

Summary

♦ Childhood experiences set the foundation for adult sexuality. For girls, adolescence is marked by ambivalence, objectification, and more restrictive sexuality. For boys, adolescence is marked by positive masculinity, physical competence, and active sexuality. The meaning and experience of first intercourse varies according to gender.

♦ The concept of sexual orientation is a social construction. Attitudes toward same-sex sexual behavior vary by culture and historical epoch. The origins of sexual orientation are unknown. The vast majority of gay men and lesbians are not confused or disturbed about their gender.

♦ Vasocongestion and myotonia are the physical processes involved in sexual response. Masters and Johnson developed a four-phase model of sexual response. Gender and culture influence various aspects of sexual response.

♦ Our beliefs underlie our sexual attitudes and behavior. Recently in Western society, there have been substantial changes in attitudes regarding women's sexuality, oral-genital sex, nonmarital sex, and same-sex relationships. Beliefs about male sexual drive and the coital imperative remain relatively unchanged.

♦ Fantasy and masturbation are the most frequent types of human sexual expression. Contemporary feminine eroticism focuses on the self as a flawed sexual object. Contemporary masculine eroticism focuses on competition and nonrelational sex. Exaggerations of the masculine erotic model contribute to coercive and exploitive sexual expression.

♦ In many societies, fertility may define womanhood and manhood. Voluntary childlessness may not be a choice. Reliable contraception has permanently changed gender relations and women's lives. Cultural forces and gender arrangements determine contraceptive practices and the availability of abortion.

♦ Sexual dysfunctions are private and subjective phenomena. The incidence and distribution of sexual dysfunctions varies by culture and gender.

♦ Pornography and prostitution are public and problematic sex-related behaviors organized along gender lines.

In-Class Activities

Lecture Suggestion:

Lecture: Bisexuality and Gender

Including bisexuality in a discussion of sexual orientation can offer unique insights into gendered sexuality. An article by Joseph Stokes, Robin Miller and Rhonda Mundhenk discusses bisexual behavior in men, while an article by Paula Rodriguez Rust discusses bisexuality and women. Both articles address the influence of culture on bisexual identity and behavior, review models of sexual orientation, and discuss issues unique to male and female bisexuals, and you may wish to refer to them if you want to address these issues in class (both are available in full text on InfoTrac). The following is a discussion of some of the gender issues brought up by a consideration of bisexuality.

The idea that men and women are "opposite" genders has contributed to a dichotomous understanding of sexual orientation. It is assumed that if a person is attracted to woman, then that person is not likely to be attracted to a man because men don't have any of the same traits that women have. Therefore, only two opposing sexualities are possible--heterosexuality and homosexuality--and bisexuality cannot exist. As a result, many people believe that bisexuals are really heterosexuals or homosexuals who are in denial, experimenting, or avoiding commitment to a particular lifestyle or partner (Rust, 2000). For example, in a survey of mostly gay males, one-third said that they "did not believe in bisexuality," (cited in Stokes et.al, 1998). This dichotomous model of sexual orientation also contributes to stereotyping of bisexuals. It is believed that since males and females are "opposites," bisexuals require sex with both genders in order to satisfy their need for both male and female qualities. Bisexuals cannot be monogamous because their needs cannot be met with just one gender at a time. In fact, few bisexuals have both male and female partners at the same time, and few feel that both male and female partners are required in order to be bisexual (Rust, 2000). (A useful analogy Rust uses to explain this point, is that a person who likes both blue-eyed and brown-eyed people is likely to be satisfied with one or the other and not feel a need for both.)

As an alternative to this dichotomous, oppositional model of sexual orientation, Stokes et al. (1998) prefer to use a model which sees attraction to men and attraction to women as two independent dimensions. In this model, a person's attraction to men does not limit his/her attraction to women. It is possible be both highly attracted to men and highly attracted to women at the same time, and knowledge of a person's sexual attractions to one gender does not tell us anything about their attractions to the other gender. Bisexuals would show some level of attraction on both dimensions. It is important to note however, that this model, is still using a gender dichotomy (attraction to males, attraction to females) to define sexual orientation. Rust (2000) makes the point that in using such a model, bisexuality is still being thought of in terms of gendered attractions—a characteristic that it not the central feature of a bisexual's sexual identity, behavior, and feelings.

Bisexuality challenges the notion that gender must be the primary factor in selection of a sexual partner. For bisexuals, a person's gender does not immediately eliminate him or her from consideration. Other factors such as a sense of humor, intelligence, physical characteristics, etc. may be more salient than gender in making a decision about a sexual or romantic partner. The reality is that men and women share most traits, and it is not inherently contradictory to experience attraction across gender. An alternative way to describe sexual orientation is in terms of a scale based on degrees of gender exclusivity—at one end, people are monosexual and base their sexual attractions on gender (heterosexual and homosexual), and at the other end people are bisexual (Rust, 2000).

It is important to note that sexual orientation is not necessarily constant across time or dimensions of sexual behavior, emotional attraction, and identity. Dichotomous, oppositional models of sexual orientation fail to capture the contradictions that are often a part of a person's sexuality. For example, Stokes et al. (1998) describe a group of men who identify as heterosexual, but who enjoy having sex with both men and women, and in some cases, only men. Rust (2000) cites research which showed that 90% of self-identified lesbians had romantic or sexual relationships with men in the past, 44% had serious heterosexual relationships (including marriage), and 43 % had been sexually involved with men since they came out as lesbians. Recognition of bisexuality forces us to broaden our view of sexuality beyond simple gendered dichotomies and should help us develop a more accurate way of defining sexual orientation.

References:

Rust, P.C.R. (2000). Bisexuality: A contemporary paradox for women. *Journal of Social Issues, 56* (2), 205-220.

Stokes, J.P., Miller, R.L, & Mundhenk, R. (1998). Toward an understanding of behaviorally bisexual men: The influence of context and culture. *The Canadian Journal of Human Sexuality, 7* (2), 101-114.

Discussion/Activity Suggestions:

1. *Activity: Exploring Gender and Sexuality Issues in Magazines.* Bring in (or ask students to bring in) magazines that are specifically directed to male or females audiences and which

address issues of sexuality (e.g., *Cosmopolitan, GQ, Men's Health, Seventeen*). Break students into small groups and give each group one men's magazine and one woman's magazine. Ask them to look at both articles and ads in the magazines for messages about sexuality. What is conveyed about feminine and masculine eroticism? Are there examples of the objectification of women? Of nonrelational sex? Of a double standard? What sexual values and norms are expressed? Are there differences between the men's magazine and the woman's magazine?

2. *Zoom and Enlarge Discussion: Contrasts and Controversies in Reproductive and Erotic Sexuality.* Box 8.2 describes how cultural traditions, gender ideology, and power can influence contraception practices. Ask students to apply a similar analysis to contraception in their own culture. How do sexual and gender norms impact the use of contraceptives? For example, how might the double standard affect contraceptive use? How might the masculine model of nonrelational sex influence contraceptive use? Why did it take so long to get pharmaceutical abortion approved in the United States? Why do we have such high rates of teen pregnancy?

3. *Discussion:* Use table 8.2 to generate a discussion about what behavior constitutes having sex. Related issues you may wish to draw out include: If coitus is the only behavior that universally counts as "sex", does that mean that gays and lesbians don't have sex? Is masturbation "sex"? Do you have to engage in "sex" to be unfaithful in a monogamous relationship? Are there gender differences in the definition of "sex"? Cultural differences? There should be a lively discussion!

4. *Discussion:* Break the class into small groups and ask them to make a list of what would change if everyone was bisexual. Have the groups report back to the class. This exercise should help students see the strong connection between gender roles and sexual behavior and attitudes. It would work especially well with the lecture on bisexuality.

Paper Assignment

Writing a Sex Education Book: Ask students to describe what information they would include in a sex education book written for young adolescents. What sexual issues would they address in the book (e.g., contraception, STD's, masturbation, sexual orientation)? What messages would they try to convey about sexuality? Would these messages be different for boys and girls? What would they tell adolescents about feminine and masculine eroticism and other cultural prescriptions for sexual behavior?

InfoTrac Exercises

1. Using the keyword search term, **contraception and gender**, find an article which explores this issue. What role does gender play in the use of contraception in this article?

2. Using the keyword search term, **adolescent sexuality**, find an article that discusses sexual decision making. What factors affect adolescents' sexual choices? Does gender play a role? Do sexual scripts or the double standard affect decision making? What are the implications of this article for helping adolescents make good decisions about their sexuality?

Test Bank for Chapter 8

Multiple Choice Questions

1. Summarize the gendered aspects of sexual development, Obj. 1, p. 165, ans. c

During adolescence, social messages regarding sexual expression
a. encourage both young men and women to inhibit their desires.
b. recognize that both young women and young men have erotic interests
c. reflect a double standard.
d. vary greatly across industrialized nations.

2. Summarize the gendered aspects of sexual development, Obj. 1, p. 165, ans. a

Surveys of middle and high school students found that
a. women expressed both positive and negative feelings about their first intercourse.
b. women described their first intercourse in very negative terms.
c. men expressed both positive and negative feelings about their first intercourse.
d. men described their first intercourse in slightly negative terms.

3. Summarize the gendered aspects of sexual development, Obj. 1, p. 165, ans. c

Which group had the lowest age of intercourse initiation in a study of teens in the U.S.?
a. Chicano males
b. Latino females
c. Black males
d. White females

4. Define *sexual orientation*, and contrast the social meaning of same-sex sexual behavior in the West with its meaning in other societies, Obj. 2, p. 166, ans. a

When it comes to same-sex sexual behavior,
a. societies vary greatly in their views of it.
b. almost all societies condemn it.
c. most Western societies have a history of tolerance for it.
d. no society currently imprisons people for it.

5. Define *sexual orientation*, and contrast the social meaning of same-sex sexual behavior in the West with its meaning in other societies, Obj. 2, p. 167, ans. d

Homosexuality was removed from the World Health Organization's International Classification of Diseases in
a. the 1960s.
b. the 1970s.
c. the 1980s.
d. the 1990s.

6. Define *sexual orientation*, Obj. 2, p. 167, ans. d

Which of the following statements about gay men and lesbians is true?
a. Gays and lesbians are not confused about their gender.
b. Social norms surrounding masculine sexuality may be exaggerated in the gay male subculture.
c. In most aspects of life, gays and lesbians resemble the heterosexual majority.
d. All of the above.

7. Summarize current findings regarding origins of sexual orientation, Obj. 3, p. 168, ans. b

Which variable correlates reliably with a same-sex orientation?
a. cross-sex behavior in childhood.
b. higher levels of education.
c. disturbed hormonal functioning.
d. differential brain structures.

8. Summarize current findings regarding origins of sexual orientation, Obj. 3, p. 169, ans. c

According to Daryl Bem's EBE theory of the development of sexual orientation, a gender nonconforming boy will experience heightened physical arousal during
a. interactions with female peers.
b. interactions with his father.
c. interactions with male peers.
d. interactions with his mother.

9. Summarize Masters and Johnson's sexual response model, Obj. 4, p. 170, ans. c

In which phase of Masters and Johnson's sexual response model does the clitoris retract under the clitoral hood?
a. excitement
b. orgasm
c. plateau
d. resolution

10. Summarize Masters and Johnson's sexual response model, Obj. 4, p. 171, ans. b

In which phase of Masters and Johnson's sexual response model is vasocongestion diffused?
a. orgasm
b. resolution
c. plateau
d. excitement

11. Summarize Masters and Johnson's sexual response model, Obj. 4, p. 171, ans. a

Which of the following is NOT a similarity in male and female sexual response?
a. a refractory period
b. myotonia
c. nipple erection
d. involuntary pelvic thrusting

12. Mention how culture influences sexual response, Obj. 4, p. 171, ans. b

Cross-cultural research indicates that
a. most areas of sexual response are remarkably similar across cultures.
b. culture can have a powerful influence on many aspects of sexual response.
c. there are no major gender differences in sexual response.
d. foreplay is the only aspect of sexual response that is influenced by culture.

13. Explain gender-related beliefs that influence sexual attitudes and behavior in Western society, Obj. 5, p. 172, ans. a

In cross-cultural comparisons of sexual permissiveness, it was found that
a. a society might be permissive in some areas, but restrictive in others.
b. there was little variation between countries.
c. attitudes in the U.S. were generally moderate.
d. no countries were permissive regarding teen sex.

14. Explain gender-related beliefs that influence sexual attitudes and behavior in Western society, Obj. 5, p. 174, ans. b

Oral-genital stimulation
a. continues to be considered a deviant behavior by most people in the United States.
b. is the most common sexual technique among same-sex couples.
c. is commonly used with prostitutes, but not generally practiced in marriage.
d. is usually less effective at producing orgasm than coitus.

15. Explain gender-related beliefs that influence sexual attitudes and behavior in Western society, Obj. 5, p. 174, ans. d

Which of the following is a consistent gender difference in sexual behavior?
a. frequency of fantasizing during partnered sex.
b. physical response to sexual arousal.
c. length of time it takes to achieve orgasm.
d. the number of partners reported.

16. Describe the central features of contemporary Western feminine and masculine eroticism, Obj. 6, p. 175, ans. c

Which of the following is NOT a gender difference in sexual fantasies?
a. imagery and content of fantasies
b. frequency of fantasy during masturbation and nonsexual activity
c. the most popular fantasies
d. age when first erotic fantasies are created

17. Describe the central features of contemporary Western feminine and masculine eroticism, Obj. 6, p. 176, ans. b

Under which circumstances is a woman LEAST likely to have an orgasm?
a. woman on top position
b. the missionary position
c. oral stimulation of the clitoris
d. manual stimulation of the clitoris

18. Describe the central features of contemporary Western feminine and masculine eroticism, Obj. 6, p. 176, ans. c

The tendency to experience sex as lust, with a minimal requirement for emotional connection is refereed to as
a. the double standard.
b. hysteria.
c. nonrelational sex.
d. the coital imperative.

19. Explain the significance of fertility and infertility and explain how gender and culture influence contraceptive use and abortion, Obj. 7, p. 177, ans. d

Infertile women
a. may be stigmatized.
b. may be punished.
c. may feel incompetent.
d. all of the above.

20. Explain the significance of fertility and infertility and explain how gender and culture influence contraceptive use and abortion, Obj. 7, p. 178, ans. b

In societies where the norm is for smaller and/or planned families, contraception is
a. a shared responsibility for men and women.
b. almost exclusively a woman's responsibility.
c. generally the responsibility of men.
d. the responsibility of the most powerful person in the relationship.

21. Explain the significance of fertility and infertility and explain how gender and culture influence contraceptive use and abortion, Obj. 7, p. 178, ans. a

When Canadian college students read a diary entry describing a sexual encounter,
a. the woman was rated more negatively when she provided a condom.
b. the man was rated more positively when he used a condom.
c. the woman was rated more positively when she provided a condom.
d. the man was rated more negatively when he did not use a condom.

22. Explain the significance of fertility and infertility and explain how gender and culture influence contraceptive use and abortion, Obj. 7, p. 179, ans. b

Around the globe,
a. unmarried women are the most likely to have an abortion.
b. high abortion rates in some countries may reflect low availability of modern contraceptives.
c. a relatively small number of women live under restrictive abortion laws.
d. illegal abortions constitute only about 25% of all abortions.

23. Describe the gender-related aspects of sexual dysfunction, Obj. 8, p. 181, ans. b

In Kaplan's model of human sexual response, where does male erectile disorder fall?
a. disorders of desire
b. disorders of arousal
c. orgasm disorder
d. plateau disorder

24. Describe the gender-related aspects of sexual dysfunction, Obj. 8, p. 182, ans. c

The most common reason why women seek the help of a sex therapist is
a. hypoactive sexual desire.
b. female arousal disorder.
c. anorgasmia.
d. sexual aversion.

25. Summarize the gender-related features of commercialized sex, Obj. 9, p. 185, ans. b

Who are the primary consumers of milder, more romanticized pornographic videos?
a. women
b. married couples
c. gay men
d. lesbians

26. Summarize the gender-related features of commercialized sex, Obj. 9, p. 185, ans. c

A prostitute is likely to
a. be careful about placing herself in risky situations.
b. use a condom when engaging in unsafe sex.
c. be an intravenous drug user.
d. all of the above.

Short-Answer Questions

27. What gender differences in sexual attitudes and experiences were revealed in surveys of middle and high school students in the U.S., Canada, and Australia?

28. Define *sexual orientation*.

29. What can we conclude about the development of a same-sex sexual orientation?

30. What are three gender differences in Masters and Johnson's sexual response model?

31. Why don't more women have orgasms during partnered sexual encounters?

32. How does the objectification of women fit into the "centerfold syndrome"?

33. What is the *motherhood mandate*?

34. Give an example of how culture can affect contraception use.

35. What is a gender difference in sexual dysfunction? Explain.

36. What are three reasons for saying that traditional hard-core pornography is problematic?

Essay Questions

36. Is there still a double standard of sexuality? What evidence supports your position?

37. What are the consequences of the nonrelational sex model for men's erotic behavior?

38. How does culture influence reproductive sexuality for women?

Chapter 9
Gender and Education

Learning Objectives

1. List and describe three important ideas relevant to understanding the relationship between gender and education.

2. Contrast the current educational practices that were described as "shortchanging" girls with the findings regarding practices that seem to harm boys.

3. Summarize how gender influences the educational process in terms of gender arrangements in the elementary grades, gendered textbooks and readers, teacher perceptions and expectations, and career preparation.

4. Summarize the major explanations for the gender imbalance in particular educational domains, and then describe the changes that have been proposed to rectify that imbalance.

5. Summarize the current findings and recommendations regarding gender and study of mathematics.

6. Summarize the current findings regarding gender and computer technology.

7. Summarize the current findings regarding the paucity of women in the physical sciences and engineering.

8. Summarize the important features of the relationship between gender and education in developing countries.

Summary

*   Education is the process by which the skills and knowledge relevant to a particular culture are learned and applied. An advanced education for all who desire it is a relatively new idea. Norms of gender, ethnicity, and social class influence educational choices and patterns. Basic literacy is still a distant goal for much of the world's population.

*   A series of reports set off a debate as to whether girls are "shortchanged" by the current educational processes. Recent findings suggest that gender-related factors in the educational process are also detrimental to boys' academic achievement.

*   The elementary school classroom is characterized by a relative absence of men teachers, by gender-stereotypic texts, and by gender-biased teacher perceptions, expectations, and attributions. There are persistent gender-related and ethnicity-related differentials in career choice and occupational preparation.

*   Difference models and deficit models have been proposed to explain the relative gender

imbalance among students in mathematics, the physical sciences, engineering, and information technology. Several reforms have attempted to rectify this gender imbalance.

♦ Women's mathematical underachievement is not a cultural universal, yet it persists in North American society and in western Europe. A number of psychosocial variables maintain computer technology as a masculine domain. Women scientists have aggregated in the life sciences. Women continue to avoid adequate academic preparation in the fields of physics, engineering, and the information sciences.

♦ Education remains a critical arena in which gender inequities may be maintained or modified. For poor nations, basic literacy and numeracy are major, but often elusive goals. Many factors combine to maintain lower literacy rates among women all over the developing world. Literacy and more years of education are often correlated with other significant social and economic benefits.

♦ In industrial and postindustrial societies, patterns of gender segregation in educational choices continue. These patterns culminate in inequities in occupational and economic achievement.

In-Class Activities

Lecture Suggestion:

Lecture: Gender and the SAT's

As a tool for making admissions decisions at many colleges, the SAT can have a profound impact on men and women's educational experience. In 1999, over 1.2 million students took the SAT (Hyde and Kling, 2001). The SAT is potentially useful because it gives colleges a uniform assessment measure with which to compare applicants from a variety of educational backgrounds. However, it also has a history of gender, racial and class bias. Janet Shibley Hyde and Kristen C. Kling discuss the impact of gender on the SAT as part of an article on women and achievement:

Males score higher on the math portion of the SAT, and the size of this gender gap has been consistent since 1972. For example in 1999, males had an average score of 531, while females scored an average of 495. There is no comparable gender gap on the verbal portion of the test. Changes were made to the test in 1972 in order to eliminate the female advantage in verbal scores. Since then, males have consistently scored slightly higher than females. In 1999, this difference was 509 for males and 502 for females.

There are a number of possible explanations for the SAT gender gap. One is that the students who take the SAT are a selective sample, and samples selected for higher ability are likely to show a larger gender difference favoring males in math. When this is combined with the greater variability in men's scores, the result is higher average scores for men. Women are also more likely to take SAT (54% female vs. 46% male in 1999), so the pool of female test takers includes a larger percentage of lower ability students, thus depressing the group average. Stereotype threat also is a likely contributor to the gender gap in math scores. The fact that the SAT is seen as a very important exam which is measuring math ability, makes it more likely that stereotype threat will be a factor and cause women (especially those who are competent in math) to perform below their potential.

On other measures of academic ability, females demonstrate greater achievement. Most significantly, they score higher grades at all levels (as is discussed in the text). In 1999, the GPA average for SAT takers was 3.31 for females, while it was 3.16 for males. Girls taking the SAT are also more likely to report having taken honors classes. Further, girls are more likely to be on the honor roll, be elected as class officers, belong to academic clubs, and engaged in community service.

The SAT does predict grades in the first year of college. However, due to the gender effect which favors males, and the fact that women get higher grades in college, the SAT underpredicts the college grades that women will earn. This female underprediction effect has been documented over last 25 years. As Hyde and Kling point out, although the magnitude of this effect is small, in the context of admissions procedures at large, competitive universities, it can negatively affect a large number of women. For example they cite a study on admissions at the University of California at Berkeley, where it was estimated that between 200 and 300 nonminority women were denied admission on the basis of the gender bias in the SAT. As a result, Hyde and Kling argue that policymakers should be concerned about the SAT's gender bias and the female underprediction effect.

References:

Hyde, J.S & Kling, K.C. (2001). Women, motivation, and achievement. *Psychology of Women Quarterly, 25* (4), 364-378.

Discussion/Activity Suggestions:

1. *Activity: Panel of Students Studying Non-Traditional Fields.* Invite students and/or faculty who have studied a field that is dominated by the other gender, to your class. his should include women who are involved in the physical sciences, computer science, math and engineering, but also men who are studying elementary or early childhood education, nursing, dance or other fields dominated by women. Before they come to class, have your students generate a list of questions to ask the panel, focusing on how the issue of gender has impacted their educational experience.

2. *Slide Show Activity: A Glimpse into Classrooms Around the Industrialized World*: Box 9.4 describes gender issues in education in several countries. You can further broaden students' understanding of cross-cultural issues in gendered education by asking them either alone or in groups, to get onto the internet and research the issue of education and gender in another country. (The terms gender, education, and the country's name entered into a search engine will produce useful hits.) Have them report their findings to the class.

3. *Discussion:* After they are familiar with the issues described in this chapter, ask students to generate all the reasons they can think of for gender segregated schooling (at all age levels and for boys and girls). Ask them to generate all the reasons they can think of for gender integrated schooling. Is gender segregation a good way to address gender issues in education? Why or why not?

Paper Assignment

Closing the Gender Gap: Ask students to imagine that they are the Secretary of Education, and write a report describing what they see as the most serious gender issues facing the educational system, and a set of recommendations for solving these issues. Remind them to address not only the issues that affect girls and women, but also those that affect boys and men.

InfoTrac Exercise

Using the keyword search, enter the term **gender** and one of the subjects described as having a gender gap (**physics, math, computer science, science**). Find an article which both discusses an area of gender difference in this field, and provides suggestions for ending the gender difference. Do the researchers take a difference or deficit approach to this gender difference? How feasible is their plan to close the gender gap?

Test Bank for Chapter 9

Multiple Choice Questions

1. Describe ideas relevant to understanding the relationship between gender and education, Obj. 1, p. 190, ans. c

During which decade did the number of women attending college in the U.S. begin to equal the number of college men?
a. the 1960s
b. the 1970s
c. the 1980s
d. the 1990s

2. Describe ideas relevant to understanding the relationship between gender and education, Obj. 1, p. 190, ans. a

From a global perspective, the privilege of basic literacy
a. is more available to boys than to girls.
b. is more available to girls than to boys.
c. is equally available to boys and girls.
d. used to be more available to boys, but now is more available to girls.

3. Contrast current educational practices concerning girls and boys, Obj. 2, p. 191, ans. c

In school,
a. males and females are equally likely to sexually harass.
b. boys are much less likely to be sexually harassed.
c. girls experience harassment as threatening while boys tend to see it as normative.
d. both boys and girls see harassment as threatening.

4. Contrast current educational practices concerning girls and boys, Obj. 2, p. 192, ans. b

Which of the following is NOT true of the education of boys?
a. Boys receive more praise, criticism, and remediation.
b. Boys get better grades.
c. Boys drop out at higher rates.
d. Boys are more likely to be labeled as emotionally or behaviorally disordered.

5. Contrast current educational practices concerning girls and boys, Obj. 2, p. 192, ans. d

Which of the following changes in education designed to benefit girls, has been harmful to boys?
a. Involving students in real-life science experiments.
b. Getting rid of harassment and bullying in the classroom and schoolyard.
c. Working to eliminate gender segregation in choice of classes and careers.
d. None of the above, when something works for one gender, it works for the other as well.

6. Summarize how gender influences education in the early grades, Obj. 3, p. 193, ans. c

On the playground,
a. boys and girls are equally likely to invade each other's spaces.
b. girls are generally tolerant of boys' aggressive behaviors, recognizing "it's all in fun".
c. girls are often ignored when they complain of boys' intrusive behaviors.
d. boys are likely to enjoy it when girls intrude or harass them.

7. Summarize how gender influences textbooks and readers, Obj. 3, p. 193, ans. b

Across cultures, it was found that schoolbooks
a. no longer portray males and females in stereotypic ways.
b. continue to communicate gender stereotypes.
c. portray women stereotypically, but not men.
d. convey messages of gender equality.

8. Summarize how gender influences teacher perceptions, Obj. 3, p. 193, ans. d

Which of the following student characteristics has been demonstrated to affect teachers' perceptions and expectations?
a. gender
b. ethnicity
c. social class
d. all of the above

9. Summarize how gender influences teacher perceptions, Obj. 3, p. 194, ans. a

In a study of academic disidentification, which of the following groups demonstrated academic disidentification across all content areas?
a. African-American boys
b. African-American girls
c. White girls
d. Both White and African-American girls

10. Summarize how gender influences teacher perceptions, Obj. 3, p. 194, ans. b

In evaluations of teachers, college students
a. were more likely to choose a woman as their "worst professor".
b. were more likely to choose a professor of their own gender as their "best professor".
c. were more likely to choose a man as their "worst professor".
d. were more likely to choose a woman as their "best professor".

11. Summarize how gender influences career preparation, Obj. 3, p. 194, ans. c

When it comes to gender differences in career preparation,
a. Girls and women are more restrictive about appropriate work preparation and selection.
b. Men have flexible self-concepts and imagine themselves in a broader array of life domains.
c. Women continue to experience greater self-efficacy in women-dominated fields.
d. Family and home responsibilities are not a consideration when men select their occupations.

12. Summarize how gender influences career preparation, Obj. 3, p. 195, ans. a

In a study of the relationship between androgyny and collegiate aspirations,
a. there was greater androgyny in the group of women studying cosmetology.
b. there was greater androgyny in the group of women who were college bound.
c. both groups had equally high levels of androgyny.
d. both groups had equally low levels of androgyny.

13. Summarize explanations for gender imbalance in math and science, Obj. 4, p. 198, ans. b

Which of the following is NOT a difference model explanation for the gender imbalance in math and science?
a. There is a persistence gap between women and men.
b. Women need to achieve a critical mass in math and science.
c. Women's ways of knowing are not suited to math and science.
d. Women experience greater demands of competing life roles.

14. Summarize explanations for gender imbalance in math and science, Obj. 4, p. 198, ans. d

If the gender imbalance in math and science is due to a "leaky pipeline", then the solution is to
a. build a critical mass of women in the scientific workplace.
b. demand that men participate equally in childcare and housework.
c. end discriminatory workplace policies.
d. socialize girls into science and math in childhood and offer them more training opportunities

15. Summarize explanations for gender imbalance in math and science, Obj. 4, p. 198, ans. c

For girls and women wishing careers in science,
a. there are excellent opportunities for research funding.
b. there is equal access to professional and social networks.
c. there is a strong likelihood of professional isolation.
d. there is a good chance of finding a mentor.

16. Summarize explanations for gender imbalance in math and science, Obj. 4, p. 199, ans. b

Women who succeed in math and science tend to
a. come from poorer families compared to the men in these fields.
b. come from families with fathers in technical or scientific occupations.
c. be graduates of large universities.
d. all of the above.

17. Summarize current findings and recommendations regarding gender and the study of mathematics, Obj. 5, p. 199, ans. d

The gender gap in math performance
a. has virtually disappeared on standardized tests.
b. is evident no matter which criteria are used.
c. exists even in elementary school.
d. varies widely across cultures.

18. Summarize current findings and recommendations regarding gender and the study of mathematics, Obj. 5, p. 200, ans. c

Which of the following strategies produces equivalent math performance in both genders?
a. competitive motivational techniques.
b. didactic instruction.
c. use of realistic and practical problems in assignments.
d. all of the above.

19. Summarize findings regarding gender and computer technology, Obj. 6, p. 201, ans. c

Which of the following statements regarding gender and computer technology is true?
a. The number of women earning college degrees in computer science has been climbing.
b. Boys and men experience lower self-efficacy in regard to computers.
c. Teachers tend to encourage boys more in the computer classroom.
d. There is no gender difference in the level of positive affect toward computers.

20. Summarize findings regarding the paucity of women in physical sciences and engineering, Obj. 7, p. 201, ans. d

When does the gender gap in science begin?
a. elementary school
b. high school
c. college
d. middle school

21. Summarize findings regarding the paucity of women in physical sciences and engineering, Obj. 7, p. 202, ans. b

When women do persist in scientific careers, they
a. tend to concentrate in the physical sciences.
b. tend to end up in the least prestigious areas.
c. are as successful as men.
d. are likely to be supported by male mentors.

22. Summarize the features of the relationship between gender and education in developing countries, Obj. 8, p. 202, ans. a

Which region of the world has the highest percentage of female illiteracy?
a. Sub-Saharan Africa
b. Middle East
c. Asia
d. Latin America

23. Summarize the features of the relationship between gender and education in developing countries, Obj. 8, p. 203, ans. b

Globally, the gender gap in literacy
a. is growing larger.
b. is slowly shrinking.
c. has remained the same for the past 25 years.
d. has almost closed.

24. Summarize the features of the relationship between gender and education in developing nations (in this case, postindustrial nations), Obj. 8, p. 206, ans. d

Which nation has a strong tradition of full gender equity in education, labor force participation and gender balance at all levels of government?
a. United Kingdom
b. Japan
c. United States
d. Sweden

25. Summarize the features of the relationship between gender and education in developing countries, Obj. 8, p. 208, ans. c

In general, the education of girls and women is correlated with
a. earlier marriage.
b. larger family size preference.
c. longer life expectancies.
d. increased fertility rates.

Short-Answer Questions

26. What role can extracurricular sports play in contributing to gender differences in education?

27. On the playground, how do boys and girls learn that boys' aggression is "natural" and must be tolerated and accommodated?

28. Why is the elementary school classroom among the most highly gender-segregated workplaces?

29. What messages about gender are conveyed by school readers and textbooks?

30. What did researchers find in a study of the occupational aspirations and expectations among inner-city boys?

31. Explain the difference between a *difference model* and a *deficit model* explanation of the low number of women in math, science and technology.

32. What are the consequences of isolation for women scientists?

33. Describe one gender difference in math that favors boys and one that favors girls.

34. How do teachers contribute to the gender gap in computer technology?

35. How does the status of agricultural production in a developing nation affect gender and education?

36. Explain why families in many traditional societies accrue greater benefits from educating boys than girls.

Essay questions

37. If you were on a university committee that was trying to increase the number of women in math and sciences majors, what recommendations would you make?

38. If you were an elementary school teacher, how would you encourage the girls in your class to participate more in science, math and computer technology? Would these programs harm or help boys? Explain.

39. Explain why basic education does not guarantee empowerment.

Chapter 10
Gender and Work

Learning Objectives

1. Describe the likely origins of the division of labor by gender, and then provide a brief overview of the history of human labor emphasizing recent social changes.

2. Describe the relationship between masculinity and success in the worker-provider role, mentioning the concept of positionality.

3. Explain three issues relevant to understanding the relationship between gender and work on a global level.

4. Explain how occupational aspirations and expectations are influenced by gender and other sociocultural factors, emphasizing recent findings across nations and within the United States.

5. List and explain seven gender-related factors relevant to the course of career path development.

6. Define and describe the nature of occupational segregation and then provide an overview of two major approaches that attempt to explain how such segregation is maintained.

7. Explain the relationships among gender stereotyping, gender discrimination, and occupational segregation, and then summarize recent findings regarding gender and compensation.

8. Explain the metaphors of the sticky floor, the glass ceiling, and the high-speed escalator, emphasizing their impact on gender-differential success in managerial positions.

9. Explain how the Tall People parable relates to the struggle for gender equity in the workplace.

10. Describe three factors relevant to understanding the relationship among gender, employment demands, and family needs.

11. Summarize the findings regarding quality of life in the contemporary dual-earner family.

12. Summarize the perspectives and policies regarding parental leave and child care across several nations.

Summary

♦ The division of the labor needed for survival according to gender is one of the most ancient, fundamental, and enduring aspects of human societies.

♦ Development of a separate masculine workplace versus a feminine home place began with the industrial revolution. Beginning in the 1960s, large numbers of middle-class women re-entered paid employment.

♦ In the industrial world, the masculine gender role centers on success in the worker and provider roles.

♦ Women's labors are often neither perceived as work, nor counted as economic productivity. Economic globalization concentrates women in low-paying jobs. All over the world women are securing low-cost loans that facilitate self-employment.

♦ Occupational segregation and its inequities begin with gender differentiated aspirations, expectations, and career development. The differential career paths of men and women are based on a number of factors.

♦ Occupational segregation by type and level of work is a prominent feature of the contemporary workplace. Gender differentials in prestige, status, advancement opportunities, and compensation all follow from this segregation. Overall, men still receive higher pay for the same work.

♦ The two major explanations for the establishment and maintenance of occupational segregation differ in terms of emphasis. Traditional psychological theories emphasize more internal, socialization-related factors. Structural theories emphasize more external and situational factors.

♦ Gender bias, stereotyping and discrimination are important and complex factors related to gender and paid work. The qualities traditionally associated with management and supervision result in a masculine bias in hiring for these positions. The sticky floor, the glass ceiling, the high-speed escalator, and the parable of the tall and short people are useful metaphors in understanding the relevant gender issues.

♦ The competing demands of job and family are prominent issues in the now normative dual-earner family. Earlier findings of greater distress among employed women were related to second-class and second-shift treatment, rather than to work itself. Across cultures, families and nations have developed varying ways of viewing and dealing with the issues of parental leave and child care.

In-Class Activities

Lecture Suggestion:

Lecture: The Experiences of African-American and White Women Firefighters

A concrete example of how gender and race/ethnicity can impact work experience can be found in a study of African-American and White women firefighters conducted by Janice Yoder and Lynne Berendsen:

Analyzing data from both a mail survey and telephone interviews, Yoder and Berendsen describe commonalties and differences in the experiences of African-American and White women firefighters. Both groups are marginalized as women in a profession dominated by men—they are "outsiders within"—members of a team (within) who exist on the fringes (outsiders). Both African-American and White women described experiences of subordination through exclusion. However, these experiences were also influenced by race/ethnicity, so there were also differences between these groups of women.

Both African-American women and White women received insufficient instruction (primarily during their initial training), and were treated with hostility by coworkers. However, there was a significant group of White women who felt they had never been victims of insufficient training or coworker hostility. This group felt that their experiences with male coworkers had been positive overall, and some expressed surprise that other women reported such incidents. None of the African-American women reported these kinds of feelings. Other methods of exclusion reported by both African-American and White women were the "silent treatment," and close and punitive supervision. White women generally reported that these methods of exclusion were more of a factor in their early years with the department, and that they declined over time. A few White women believed that these were just "initiation rites" which were part of every novice's training and were unrelated to gender. African-American women on the other hand, reported a pattern that lasted for years and eventually led to self-withdrawal as they gave up hoping for acceptance.

Both groups also experienced exclusion through stereotyping and differential treatment. Race as well as gender influenced these stereotypes. African-American women had to contend with stereotypes of themselves as welfare recipients and "beasts of burden," who were expected to do more work and carry heavier loads. In contrast, White women were stereotyped and treated as though they were fragile and required paternal overprotection. They tried to counteract this stereotype by working ceaselessly and covering up injuries. While African-American women had to deal with over-burdening, White women had to deal with under-burdening.

Both African-American and White women felt that affirmative action had helped them get hired, neither felt that it harmed their own feelings of competence, but both groups felt that affirmative action undermined others' confidence in their abilities. Further, both groups felt persistently pressured to prove their physical strength, loyalty to their team, and fire fighting knowledge. They saw this strong pressure as lasting throughout their fire fighting careers.

Yoder and Berendsen point out that while these two groups of women share many similar experiences, their racial/ethnic differences have the potential to create misunderstanding and disunity between the groups. They argue that African-American women may be subordinated through exclusion, while White women are subordinated through seduction—through the privileged racial status they share with White men. This was evident in the reports of some White women who saw themselves as "one of the guys," and reported no negative treatment. The bonds White women share with White men may also make it possible to overcome their initial exclusionary treatment. These options did not seem to be available to the African American women.

References:

Yoder, J.D. & Berendsen, L.L. (2001). "Outsider within" the firehouse: African American and White women firefighters. *Psychology of Women Quarterly, 25* (1), 27-36.

Discussion/Activity Suggestions:

1. *Slide Show Activity: Engendering Specific Occupations.* Box 10.1 looks at gender segregation in a variety of occupations. You can begin your discussion of gender segregation in the workplace by asking each person in class to state the various jobs they have held in their lives. Gender segregation will be apparent as you go around the group. Ask the class what trends they saw in the list of jobs. If there are people who have done work that was nontraditional for their gender, you may wish to ask them how their gender played a role in their experiences with that job.

2. *Zoom and Enlarge Activity: Men in the World of Women's Work.* Invite a panel of men and women

working in nontraditional occupations to class. Box 10.2 describes some of the differences in what men and women experience when they participate in a nontraditional job. Ask panelists about their experiences both in and out of the workplace: Do they experience prejudice inside their workplace? Outside of their workplace? How do they feel about being more visible at work because of their gender? Have they been able to find a mentor? How have they done in terms of promotion and salary compared to others at their job? This activity would also work well with the lecture on women firefighters.

3. *ABCs of Gender Activity: The Issue: Gender and Work.* There are a number of activities you can do with the questionnaire in Box. 10.4. You can ask the class to fill it out, collect it, and report on the findings. You can suggest that students in committed romantic relationships fill it out with their partner. Ask them to report to the class on whether or not it was useful to do this with their partners. You can ask the class to make copies of the questionnaire and give it out to a male and a female. What differences, if any, did they find in the answers?

4. *Discussion:* Ask students to talk about how the workplace would change if there was true gender equity.

Paper Assignment

Analyzing a Career from the Perspective of Gender: Ask students to read an autobiography of a man or a woman who succeeded at a nontraditional job, and then analyze his or her career in terms of gender-related work issues. Some questions they might answer include: How did this work affect his sense of masculinity? Was the path of career development affected by gender? What experiences did the person have as someone who worked in a nontraditional environment? Did the person experience tokenism? Did the person experience stereotyping or discrimination in their career? Any examples of the glass ceiling, glass escalator, or sticky floor? How did the person fit family into his or her career? Does this person's experience support or refute the material covered in this chapter?

InfoTrac Exercise

Using the one of the keyword search terms **occupational segregation, glass ceiling,** or **sticky floor**, find an article which uses *qualitative* methods to research the impact of this gender issue at work. Does qualitative research add something to your understanding of this issue? Explain.

Test Bank for Chapter 10

Multiple Choice Questions

1. Describe the likely origins of the division of labor by gender, Obj. 1, p. 213, ans. b

The origin of the division of labor by gender
a. was likely arbitrary.
b. was the result of differences in physical strength and child-related responsibilities.
c. is unclear.
d. differs from society to society.

2. Provide an overview of the history of human labor, Obj. 1, p. 213, ans. d

In hunting-and-gathering societies, women's work
a. is primarily devoted to childcare and cooking.
b. is the same as men's work.
c. is secondary to the hunting and defense work done by men.
d. provides about 80% of needed food.

3. Provide an overview of the history of human labor, Obj. 1, p. 213, ans. c

During World War II
a. the notion of separate spheres for men and women was developed.
b. women's wages were viewed as supplemental and secondary.
c. women worked in factories at every level of manufacturing and management.
d. the decline in manufacturing and the rise in service occupations created more jobs for women.

4. Provide an overview of the history of human labor, Obj. 1, p. 214, ans. d

In the United States today,
a. the majority of paid workers are still men.
b. the workforce is made up of equal numbers of men and women.
c. the number of women working for wages has diminished significantly.
d. women comprise well over half the workforce.

5. Describe the relationship between masculinity and success in the worker-provider role, Obj. 2, p. 215, ans. c

Which of the following is NOT true of masculinity and the worker role?
a. Most men continue to define themselves primarily by and through their work.
b. Mainstream masculinity is equated with ambition, power and authority.
c. Unlike girls' play, sports and traditional masculine play do not prepare boys for future work roles.
d. The chronically unemployed or underachieving man loses status and identity as an adequate male.

6. Describe the relationship between masculinity and success in the worker-provider role, Obj. 2, p. 216, ans. a

Why doesn't their work role make most men feel very successful?
a. because masculinity is defined through positionality
b. because they neglect their families in favor of work
c. because their partners are not supportive
d. because gender segregation limits their job choices

7. Explain three issues relevant to understanding the relationship between gender and work on a global level, Obj. 3, p. 217, ans. c

All over the world, women's traditional labors
a. are considered part of the formal labor sector.
b. are counted as part of a nation's gross national product.
c. have not been counted as an economic activity.
d. are considered to be "real work" even though they are unpaid.

8. Explain three issues relevant to understanding the relationship between gender and work on a global level, Obj. 3, p. 217, ans. d

What percentage of light-weight assembly workers in the garment and electronics industries are women?
a. 10 percent
b. 25 percent
c. 50 percent
d. 90 percent

9. Explain how occupational aspirations are influenced by gender and other sociocultural factors, Obj. 4, p. 218, ans. a

In a study of adolescents from 11 nations, the relatively low level of social welfare supports in eastern Europe and the United States may explain why youth from these countries
a. emphasized the importance of taking responsibility for their families.
b. emphasized the importance of social pleasure.
c. defined success more in terms of fame, money and professionalism.
d. showed more interest in future education and careers.

10. Explain how occupational aspirations are influenced by gender and other sociocultural factors, Obj. 4, p. 218, ans. c

Studies of high school students which compared young women and young men found that
a. among academic risk students, young women were more occupationally discouraged.
b. among academic risk students, young men aspired to higher-prestige occupations.
c. among gifted students, young women tended to lower their occupational aspirations in adolescence.
d. among gifted students, young men were more conflicted regarding their career interests.

11. Explain how occupational aspirations are influenced by gender and other sociocultural factors, Obj. 4, p. 218, ans. b

When college students were asked to rate the importance of success in various life domains,
a. there was a substantial amount of disagreement between males and females.
b. there was considerable consensus across race, gender and class categories.
c. white students rated economic success as more important than did students of color.
d. working class students attached more importance to attaining family goals than middle class students.

12. List and explain gender-related factors relevant to the course of career path development, Obj. 5, p. 219, ans. b

When it comes to women's path of career development,
a. women with more instrumental and expressive traits are more likely to choose traditional occupations.
b. women's occupational choices may be influenced by a spouses' occupational choices.
c. women's career aspirations are now equal to or higher than men's aspirations.
d. all of the above.

13. List and explain gender-related factors relevant to the course of career path development, Obj. 5, p. 219, ans. a

Gender differences in salary
a. persist, even when education, age, experience and performance are taken into account.
b. have been eliminated.
c. are not apparent in lifetime wages.
d. disappear when education, age, experience and performance are taken into account.

14. Describe the nature of occupational segregation, Obj. 6, p. 220, ans. c

Compared to men, women
a. typically have more workplace authority.
b. are employed in a wider range of occupations and industries.
c. aggregate in occupations characterized by lower status.
d. earn similar compensation if they are in a similar occupational category.

15. Provide an overview of two approaches which explain how gender segregation is maintained, Obj. 6, p. 221, ans. c

Which of the following is NOT an internal explanation of occupational segregation?
a. gender differences in communication styles.
b. gender differences in intrinsic and extrinsic work values
c. existence of a wage penalty for workers in female-dominated occupations.
d. gender socialization which makes women experience workplace events as more stressful than do men.

16. Provide an overview of two approaches which explain how gender segregation is maintained, Obj. 6, p. 221, ans. c

With overall lower pay, prestige, and authority, women
a. are likely to report slightly lower levels of job satisfaction than men.
b. generally report similar levels of job satisfaction when compared to men.
c. often report greater levels of job satisfaction than do men.
d. are likely to report much lower levels of job satisfaction than men.

17. Explain the relationships among gender stereotyping, gender discrimination, and occupational segregation, Obj. 7, p. 225, ans. d

Gender stereotyping has been shown to affect
a. employee selection.
c. performance evaluations.
d. self-perceptions.
d. all of the above.

18. Summarize findings regarding gender and compensation, Obj. 7, p. 225, ans. d

Studies of self-pay expectations have shown that
a. in women-dominated fields such as nursing and education, women expect more pay than do men.
b. women expect lower pay than men at entry but comparable pay at their projected career peak.
c. in men-dominated fields such as engineering, women expect more pay than do men.
d. in all fields, women expect lower pay than men both at entry and at their projected career peak.

19. Explain how the sticky floor, glass ceiling and the high-speed escalator impact on success in managerial positions, Obj. 8, p. 226, ans. c

In a study comparing male and female executives, it was found that
a. women managers managed more subordinates.
b. male managers received fewer stock options.
c. women managers had less workplace authority.
d. there were no gender differences in workplace authority, number of subordinates, and stock options.

20. Explain how the sticky floor, glass ceiling and the high-speed escalator impact on success in managerial positions, Obj. 8, p. 226, ans. d

In a study of manager turnover in Fortune 500 firms, it was found that
a. there was higher turnover among men than women.
b. women had higher turnover than men because of family issues.
c. there was no gender difference in turnover rates.
d. women had higher turnover than men because of job dissatisfaction.

21. Explain how the sticky floor, glass ceiling and the high-speed escalator impact on success in managerial positions, Obj. 8, p. 226, ans. b

The obstacles women face in advancing to supervisory and management roles is called
a. the glass ceiling.
b. the sticky floor.
c. the high-speed escalator.
d. the stuck elevator.

22. Explain how the sticky floor, glass ceiling and the high-speed escalator impact on success in managerial positions, Obj. 8, p. 227, ans. c

When men cross the boundary into occupations traditionally occupied by women, they face
a. the glass ceiling.
b. the sticky floor.
c. the high-speed escalator.
d. the stuck elevator.

23. Describe three factors relevant to understanding the relationship among gender, employment demands, and family needs, Obj. 10, p. 229, ans. c

Fathers with a "double shift," report
a. less stress than mothers with a double shift.
b. more stress than mothers with a double shift.
c. the same level of stress as mothers with a double shift.
d. fathers don't have double shifts.

24. Describe three factors relevant to understanding the relationship among gender, employment demands, and family needs, Obj. 10, p. 229, ans. b

A friend claims that women choose lower-level jobs because they give higher priority to raising a family. How do you respond?
a. "You're right, traditionally man-dominated jobs are the least amenable to raising a family."
b. "You're wrong, traditionally woman-dominated jobs are the least amenable to raising a family."
c. "You're right, single women do not choose such jobs."
d. "You're wrong, married men give higher priority to raising a family too."

25. Summarize findings regarding quality of life in the dual-earner family, Obj. 11, p. 231, ans. d

Employed women in dual-earner families
a. generally experience poorer physical health compared to full-time homemakers.
b. see work as the most important issue in their lives.
c. experience an equitable division of household labor.
d. have more cooperative and collaborative relationships with their partners.

26. Summarize the policies regarding parental leave and child care across nations, Obj. 12, p. 233, ans. a

Which country has the best parental leave policy?
a. Sweden
b. China
c. United States
d. Canada

27. Summarize the policies regarding parental leave and child care across nations, Obj. 12, p. 233, ans. a

Which country does NOT consider child care a private parental responsibility?
a. France
b. Canada
c. United States
d. Britain

Short-Answer Questions

28. What were the emerging gender ideals for women and men in the 1950s?

29. Define *positionality*.

30. Explain the statement that "all over the world women's traditional labors have not been constructed as real work at all" (p. 217).

31. Describe two issues that must be consider when trying to understand the path of career development in both women and men.

32. Give three examples of occupational segregation.

33. Are there gender differences in intrinsic and extrinsic work values? Explain.

34. What is the difference between the "sticky floor," the "glass ceiling," and "the high speed escalator"?

35. What workplace conditions help working parents experience less stress and better work outcomes?

36. What are two benefits of being a member of a dual-earner family?

37. How does the view that child care is a community issue affect child care practices?

Essay Questions

38. What have been the effects of the feminization of the postindustrial workforce?

39. What is problematic for men in defining masculinity through work?

40. How can gender stereotyping contribute to occupational segregation?

41. Explain how the Tall People parable relates to the struggle for gender equity in the workplace.

Chapter 11
Gender and Physical Health

Learning Objectives

1. Offer a brief history of gender-related factors in health, illness, and treatment, mentioning the accomplishments of the women's health movement.

2. List and explain three important contemporary issues related to gender and health.

3. Explain what is meant by the gender-related context of health, offering examples of how gender influences (a) the health problems individuals are likely to have, (b) interactions with health care providers, (c) the structure and functioning of the health care system, and (d) culture-related health factors.

4. Explain how gender influences occupational and reproductive health difficulties.

5. List and explain the major gender-related lifestyle factors that influence patterns of health and illness, paying special attention to sexual lifestyles in the industrial and postindustrial nations and in Africa.

6. Explain the gender-related central paradox regarding morbidity and longevity, and summarize the hypothesized explanations for this phenomenon.

7. Summarize the gender-related factors surrounding coronary disease.

8. Summarize the gender-related factors surrounding cerebral vascular accidents, cancer, and dementia.

Summary

♦ In past centuries, infectious diseases were the major threats to health. Beginning in the 18th century, women were gradually excluded from the healing arts and from participating in the development of modern medical science. Women's health movement activists have improved gender-relevant health services in many areas.

♦ Contemporary concerns include (a) the importance of understanding gender-related health issues, (b) the distortions and stereotypes perpetuated by "racial" classifications in the organization and presentation of health data, (c) making health data understandable to the lay public, and (d) adequate health care on a global scale.

♦ Health promotion, illness, and the health service system all exist in a complex and highly gendered context or framework. Gender affects virtually every aspect of health, including the biological bases of pathology, medical education, the medical research system, the delivery of health services, and the dissemination of health information.

♦ Job-related factors no longer pose the health threat they once did, but boys and men are still more likely to sustain injuries and illnesses in the workplace. In more industrialized societies, pregnancy and childbirth are safe processes. In the developing world, however, reproductive processes pose a major health threat for women and children. Overall, women still lack the power to influence social policies regarding reproductive health.

♦ In industrialized societies, most illness is caused by behavior and decision-making processes. Key elements of traditional Western masculinity are associated with high rates of injury and illness. Sports injuries, interpersonal aggression, vehicular accidents, tobacco use, substance abuse, unprotected sex with multiple partners, firearms use, high-fat diets, and so forth all contribute to higher morbidity and mortality rates among men. Lifestyle-related threats to women's health include smoking, substance abuse, unprotected sex with multiple partners, experiences of abuse, and eating disorders. In general, women experience greater morbidity. Moreover, caretaking of those who are ill, disabled, or dying is a traditional feminine role.

♦ In industrial societies, women use the medical system more, are ill more often, and tend to have more chronic conditions. Yet women have a longer life expectancy. Explanations for the gender gap in mortality tend to emphasize either biological factors or gender role issues.

♦ Contrary to popular belief, coronary disease is the major cause of death for both genders, but there is a gender differential in terms of when in the life span these conditions have a maximum impact on mortality.

♦ Cancer affects men and women at different points in the life span, with reproductive cancers peaking after menopause for women. For men, all types of cancer increase after age 60. Gendered lifestyle factors, especially tobacco and alcohol use, influence the types of cancers developed. Because more women live into very old age, more women develop dementias.

In-Class Activities

Lecture Suggestion:

Lecture: Gender and Physical Disability

The relationship between gender and the body is brought into sharp focus by looking at the experiences of men and women with physical disabilities. As Gerschick (2000) points out, our bodies play a key role in our recognition as appropriately gendered beings. We use our bodies to display gender (for examples, in our haircuts, physical appearance, clothing), and we physically enact gender roles (for example, in sexual practices, posture, sports). Because the body is so closely linked to the enactment of gender, physical disability can make a person vulnerable to being denied recognition as a woman or a man. Disabled women face a double burden of oppression due to ableism and sexism, and for men, disability erodes much of masculine privilege.

In the United States (and elsewhere), physical attractiveness is important in determining social and sexual desirability. Because standards of attractiveness are narrowly defined, people with physical disabilities may be seen as unattractive and therefore experience limited opportunities to care and be cared for, find love, and become parents (Gerschick, 2000 and Lisi, 1993). Physical attractiveness is viewed as especially important in determining women's desirability, and research has shown that women are four times as likely as men to divorce after developing a disability, and only 1/3 to 1/4 as likely to marry (Gerschick, 2000.)

Disability can also affect a person's participation in sport and physical fitness activities. Blinde and McCallister (1999) point out that the gender gap in participation in sports is greater for disabled women than disabled men due to double barrier of disability and the traditional feminine role. Men with disabilities, on the other hand, must contend with the traditional masculine role expectations that demand that men be competitive and physically strong. These attributes are often demonstrated through participation in sports, but disabilities may make such participation difficult or even impossible.

People with disabilities experience greater rates of abuse. For example, children with disabilities are 70 percent more likely to be physically or sexually abused. The forms of abuse follow gendered patterns, disabled women are more likely to experience sexual assault, while disabled men are more likely to experience physical assault (Gerschick, 2000). Disabled people are also more economically vulnerable, and again this is influenced by gender. For example, U.S. Census statistics indicate that in 1994 labor force participation for women was 74.5 percent, while it was 89.9 percent for men. For women with mild disabilities, participation dropped to 68.4 percent, while for men it was 85.1 percent. For women and men with severe disabilities, participation was 24.7 percent and 27.8 percent respectively (Gerschick, 2000).

An example of how disabled people meet the challenges of establishing gender identity is found in a study by Gerschick and Miller (1994). These researchers interviewed men with disabilities and found three patterns of constructing masculinity:

1) Reliance pattern. This construction of masculinity affirms the traditional male gender role. The emphasis is on control, independence, strength, and concern for appearances. In this pattern, disabled men try to compensate or overcompensate for internalized feelings of inadequacy as men. For example, they may avoid asking for help in order to meet masculine ideal of independence.

2) Reformulation pattern. Disabled men who rely on this pattern attempt to reshape traditional masculinity to fit with their own abilities, perceptions and strengths. These men do not overtly contest masculinity standards, but recognize that they are limited in their ability to achieve these standards, so they develop alternatives. For example, they may reformulate the masculine ideal of independence by hiring personal care assistants whose behavior they can direct.

3) Rejection pattern. In this pattern, disabled men believe the dominant conception of masculinity is wrong, so they develop new standards of masculinity or deny masculinity's importance. Rather than seeing themselves as deviating from the norm of masculinity, they see social constructions of masculinity as problematic. Similarly, they recognize that disability as a social construction too. Men who used this pattern saw letting go of gender expectations as a way to gain greater strength and control over their lives.

Because men and women with disabilities may have to define themselves outside of traditional gender roles, they have a unique opportunity to create new possibilities. As one disabled woman put it, "I think we are the only group of people who are trying to push that broadening of acceptance beyond culture and race, toward a broadening acceptance for everybody...that would free men and women from the stereotypes of how men and women need to be emotionally or physically," (Lisi, 1993, p. 207).
References:

Blinde, E.M. & McCallister, S.G. (1999). Women, disability, and sport and physical fitness activity: The intersection of gender and disability dynamics. *Research Quarterly for Exercise and Sport, 70* (3), 303-318.

Lisi, D. (1993). Found voices: Women, disability and cultural transformation. *Women and Therapy, 14* (3/4), 195-209.

Gerschick, T.J. (2000). Toward a theory of disability and gender. *Signs, 25* (4), 1263-1269.

Gerschick, T.J. & Miller, A.S. (1994). Coming to terms: Masculinity and physical disability. In M.S. Kimmel and M.A. Messner, (Eds.), *Men's Lives* (5th ed.), (pp.313-336). Boston: Allyn and Bacon.

Discussion/Activity Suggestions:

1. *Activity: Develop a Men's Health Program:* Break students into small groups and ask them to develop a program to improve the health practices of men on their campus. Ask them to consider health issues that are associated with the male gender role, and design an intervention which will address these issues. Have each group present their ideas to the class.

2. *Activity: Invite a Midwife to Class:* If you wish to address the medicalization of pregnancy and childbirth, a good way to do this is to invite a midwife to address your class. You can find a listing of midwives at www.

3. *Slide Show Activity: Gender, Health, Illness, and Cultural Diversity in the United States:* Box 11.3 describes gendered health issues in five different cultures (but for the purposes of this exercise, leave out the Asian American discussion). Divide the class into four small groups and assign each group one of the cultures. Ask the group to develop a program to deal with that culture's health issue. They should address the following questions in designing their program: What are the health problems that need to be addressed? What are the underlying causes of these health problems? What preventative and treatment programs are needed to solve these health problems?

4. *Discussion:* Ask students to think about how sexual gender norms can impact upon safe sex behavior. What gender norms should be taken into account when designing safe sex programs? How might safe sex programs be different for men and women?

Paper Assignment

Health Assessment: Ask students to write an assessment of their own health from the perspective of gender. What gendered health issues will they need to address during their lives? How might their health be impacted by a gendered health care system? What gendered aspects of lifestyle may affect their health? After they have done an assessment, students should conclude their paper with a plan for promoting their own health as a woman or a man.

InfoTrac Exercise

Using the keyword search, enter the term **reproductive health**. Find one article on reproductive health in a more industrial country and one article on reproductive health in a developing country. What issues are seen as key to reproductive health in each of these countries? Are there similarities is the issues addressed? Differences? What roles do culture and economic conditions play in reproductive health?

Test Bank for Chapter 11

Multiple Choice Questions

1. Offer a brief history of gender-related factors in health, Obj. 1, p. 239, ans. b

Which of the following was NOT characteristic of medicine's view of women during the Victorian era?
a. virtually all of women's ills were attributed to disorders of the female reproductive organs.
b. the upper class woman was seen as stronger and less vulnerable than lower class women.
c. men's bodies were the norm and women's bodies were seen as the exception and "abnormal."
d. medical texts contained anatomical drawings of female structures that were often inaccurate.

2. Offer a brief history of gender-related factors in health, Obj. 1, p. 240, ans. d

The women's health movement began in
a. the 1990s.
b. the 1980s.
c. the 1970s.
d. the 1960s.

3. Offer a brief history of gender-related factors in health, Obj. 1, p. 240, ans. d

Which of the following is an achievement of the women's health movement?
a. bringing attention to the problem of unnecessary cesarean sections.
b. the "patient package insert".
c. emergence of women-controlled health centers.
d. all of the above.

4. Explain contemporary issues related to gender and health, Obj. 2, p. 242, ans. c

Racial descriptors in health data records
a. are a useful way to assess health risks.
b. work well for white people, but are flawed when used with Asians.
c. distort the role social class plays in health.
d. obscure gender differences in health.

5. Explain contemporary issues related to gender and health, Obj. 2, p. 242, ans. b

Health studies that contradict accepted norms
a. quickly gain widespread acceptance.
b. tend to disappear from public awareness.
c. take hold slowly, but eventually become popular.
d. are more likely to be acclaimed by women than men.

6. Explain how gender influences the health problems individuals are likely to have, Obj. 3, p. 242, ans. a

Compared to women, men
a. are less likely to perceive themselves as vulnerable to illness.
b. have higher physical illness rates.
c. take more disability days.
d. seek care even when healthy.

7. Explain how gender influences interactions with health care providers, Obj. 3, p. 243, ans. b

In the health care system of the United States,
a. the majority of doctors and health workers are women.
b. the majority of doctors are men, but the majority of health workers are women.
c. almost half of the doctors and the majority of health workers are women.
d. half of the health workers are men.

8. Explain how gender influences interactions with health care providers, Obj. 3, p. 244, ans. c

Which medical specialty has the largest percentage of women?
a. family practice
b. psychiatry
c. ob/gyn
d. general surgery

9. Explain how gender influences interactions with health care providers, Obj. 3, p. 244, ans. a

Research on gender and communication patterns between doctors and patients reveal that
a. physicians of both genders interact more with female patients.
b. male patients ask more questions, disclose more personal information and generally talk more.
c. female physicians use more technical terms and jargon and make less eye contact.
d. male physicians use more "we" talk.

10. Explain how gender influences the structure and functioning of the health care system, Obj. 3, p. 244, ans. a

When looking at how medical research is funded, conducted and published, we find that
a. gender enters into every stage of the medical research process.
b. gender is a factor in some stages of the medical research process.
c. gender is no longer a significant factor in the medical research process.
d. gender is a factor in most stages of the medical research process.

11. Explain how gender influences culture-related health factors, Obj. 3, p. 246, ans. c

SUNDS,
a. happens primarily to women and may be related to the loss of the traditional female role.
b. happens equally to both men and women and may be due to the stress of immigration.
c. happens primarily to men and may be related to the loss of the traditional masculine role.
d. happens with greater frequency as immigrants remain in the United States.

12. Explain how gender influences culture-related health factors, Obj. 3, p. 248, ans. a

For Muslims living in Israel,
a. women's mortality was greater during the month of Ramadan than in the month after.
b. men's mortality was greater during the month of Ramadan than in the month after.
c. women's mortality was higher in the two weeks after Ramadan.
d. men's mortality was higher in the two weeks before Ramadan.

13. Explain how gender influences occupational and reproductive health difficulties, Obj. 4, p. 245, ans. b

For both men and women, the risk of coronary disease is increased when
a. the psychological demands of a job are low, and there is a great deal of individual control.
b. the psychological demands of a job are high, and there is little individual control.
c. the psychological demands of a job are low, and there is little individual control.
d. the psychological demands of a job are high, and there is a great deal of individual control.

14. Explain how gender influences occupational and reproductive health difficulties, Obj. 4, p. 247, ans. c

Strong pronatalist policies in Romania resulted in
a. a decrease in illegal abortions.
b. a decline in infant and maternal mortality.
c. institutions filled with abandoned and neglected children.
d. all of the above.

15. Explain major gender-related lifestyle factors that influence health and illness, Obj. 5, p. 249, ans. c

In North America, about _____ of the mortality from the 10 leading causes of death can be traced to aspects of lifestyle.
a. 10%
b. 25%
c. 50%
d. 75%

16. Explain major gender-related lifestyle factors that influence health and illness, Obj. 5, p. 250, ans. a

In general, traditional masculinity
a. appears to be unhealthy.
b. produces a healthy coping style.
c. is healthier than traditional femininity.
d. does not have an impact on health.

17. Explain major gender-related lifestyle factors that influence health and illness, Obj. 5, p. 250, ans. b

Compared to women, men
a. are more likely to notice symptoms of illness.
b. are less likely to have annual physicals.
c. are more likely to have nonfatal chronic conditions.
d. are less likely to experience life threatening health problems.

18. Explain major gender-related lifestyle factors that influence health and illness, Obj. 5, p. 251, ans. c

When comparing men and women in terms of alcohol abuse, we find that
a. the occurrence of drinking-related problems is about the same.
b. there are a greater number of women in alcohol treatment programs.
c. at all age levels and within all ethnic groups, men are more likely to drink heavily.
d. alcoholic men are at a greater risk of early death.

19. Explain major gender-related lifestyle factors that influence health and illness, Obj. 5, p. 252, ans. a

Which of the following gender-related lifestyle factors is more likely to apply to women?
a. weight control
b. risk-taking behavior
c. tobacco use
d. sports-related injuries

20. Explain major gender-related lifestyle factors that influence health and illness, Obj. 5, p. 253, ans. d

Which of the following statements regarding gender and HIV/AIDS is true?
a. The first symptoms of AIDS are different for men and women.
b. Woman-to-man transmission is more common than man-to-woman transmission.
c. Information about the transmission of AIDS and HIV is sufficient to change behavior.
d. Masculine and feminine sexual norms have contributed to the spread of HIV and AIDS.

21. Explain major gender-related lifestyle factors that influence health and illness, Obj. 5, p. 253, ans. d

Which of the following factors contribute to the likelihood of condom use?
a. power differences
b. gender norms
c. cultural norms
d. all of the above

22. Explain major gender-related lifestyle factors that influence health and illness, Obj. 5, p. 255, ans. a

Which region of the world has the highest number of deaths due to AIDS?
a. Sub-Saharan Africa
b. North America
c. South and Southeast Asia
d. Latin America

23. Explain the gender-related paradox regarding morbidity and longevity, Obj. 6, p. 257, ans. b

In the United States, which group can expect to live the longest?
a. White men
b. White women
c. Black men
d. Black women

24. Explain the gender-related paradox regarding morbidity and longevity, Obj. 6, p. 257, ans. c

The gender gap in longevity may be explained by
a. the protective influence of testosterone.
b. the small-scale use of hormone replacement therapy.
c. the gender norm that women seek help in the face of difficulties.
d. the gender norm that men reap the benefits of women's labor

25. Summarize gender-related factors surrounding coronary disease, Obj. 7, p. 258, ans. c

What is the number one killer of women in the United States?
a. breast cancer
b. strokes
c. coronary disease
d. lung cancer

26. Summarize gender-related factors surrounding coronary disease, Obj. 7, p. 258, ans. d

Which of the following is NOT a gender difference in coronary disease?
a. Men are more likely to be quickly referred from primary care to a cardiologist.
b. Health care workers are less likely to suspect a heart attack among women.
c. Women tend to have heart attacks much later in life than do men.
d. Men are less likely to participate in cardiac rehabilitation programs.

27. Summarize the gender-related factors surrounding cerebral vascular accidents, cancer, and dementia, Obj. 8, p. 259, ans. c

Compared to middle-aged men, middle-aged women
a. are more likely to experience a heart attack.
b. are more likely to experience a stroke.
c. are more likely to experience cancer.
d. all of the above.

28. Summarize the gender-related factors surrounding cerebral vascular accidents, cancer, and dementia, Obj. 8, p. 259, ans. b

In terms of cancer,
a. the lifetime incidence probability is higher for women than men.
b. the total mortality rate of men is double that of women.
c. women have higher rates of cancer with known causes.
d. between the ages of 15 and 34, women are more likely to die of cancer than men.

Short-Answer Questions

29. Name a major achievement of the women's health movement.

30. Why are women called the "health brokers" of the family?

31. Why are male physicians more likely to be sued than female physicians?

32. Why are adolescent boys more likely to sustain work injuries than adolescent girls?

33. Why is it important for women to be able to control their fertility?

34. Are there gender differences in tobacco use? Explain.

35. What are the possible health consequences of sexual harassment?

36. Name a cultural or gender norm in Zimbabwe that contributes to the transmission of HIV/AIDS.

37. What is the central paradox regarding gender, morbidity, and mortality?

38. Why is the perception that heart disease is a man's disease "both wrong and dangerous" (p.258)?

Essay questions

39. How does the masculine gender role contribute to health problems for men?

40. How do gendered behaviors and lifestyles affect the transmission of HIV and AIDS?

41. What changes might occur in health and illness if there was equality between women and men?

Chapter 12
Gender and Mental Health

Learning Objectives

1. List and explain two traditional concepts that are relevant to understanding the relationship between gender and psychopathology.

2. Summarize the findings related to gender and ethnic biases and the potential for stereotyping in labeling behavior as psychopathological.

3. Explain why women have been viewed as more vulnerable to mental disorder, and then explain why men have recently become more numerous in psychiatric populations.

4. Summarize current thinking about gay and lesbian mental health.

5. Explain the distinction between universally recognized patterns of disordered behavior and culture-bound syndromes, mentioning the influence of gender in six specific culture-bound syndromes.

6. Summarize the relevant data supporting the notion of eating disorders (especially anorexia) as a culture-bound syndrome, mentioning the prevalence of eating disorder in the African-American community and among men.

7. Summarize the factors believed to contribute to the greater incidence of depression among women.

8. Summarize the factors believed to contribute to the greater incidence of substance abuse among men.

9. Summarize the findings regarding the relationship between gender and anxiety disorders.

10. Summarize the findings regarding the relationship between gender and antisocial personality disorder.

11. Summarize the findings regarding gender differences in schizophrenia.

Summary

- Two notions have influenced traditional thinking about gender, mental health, and mental illness. The first was the supposed contrast between the rational man versus the irrational woman. The second was the notion that women's minds and mental functioning were totally subordinated to their reproductive functions.

- Traditional gender biases in the detection and diagnosis of psychopathology have declined, but the biases and stresses surrounding ethnicity, minority status, and poverty appear to persist in a variety of cultures.

- The behaviors designated as psychopathological have varied over time. The stereotype of women's greater vulnerability to psychopathology continues for a number of reasons, but this is changing as the number of men classified as having significant psychiatric impairment increases.

- Some patterns of behavior are universally recognized as disordered, whereas certain other patterns of behavior may be designated culture-bound syndromes. Eating disorders, especially anorexia, may be usefully viewed as a culture-bound syndrome.

- Most forms of depression are at least twice as prevalent among women, and this has been attributed to physiological, social, and individual factors. Traditional feminine gender norms facilitate high affect, high self-awareness, and a more ruminative cognitive style.

- Substance abuse is about five to six times more prevalent among men, and has been attributed to physiological, social, and individual factors. Traditional masculine gender norms facilitate denial, avoidance, and a more active, distracting cognitive style.

- Women predominate in almost all anxiety disorders, but the rates of anxiety disorders vary across nations.

- Men predominate in antisocial personality disorder, although gender bias may be at work here.

- There are significant gender variations in the findings surrounding schizophrenia. These include neuroanatomical differences, as well as differential developmental and behavioral patterns.

In-Class Activities

Lecture Suggestion:

Lecture: Gendered Therapy with Women and Men

As part of your presentation on gender and mental health, you may wish to address therapeutic techniques which specifically focus on the role gender plays in the lives of clients. Articles by Laura Brown and Annette Brodsky on feminist therapy, and Gary Brooks on a gender-sensitive approach to counseling traditional men, offer some ideas of what an explicitly "gendered" therapy can look like. In general, these therapies share the belief that individual psychology is shaped by a gendered social context which limits and harms individuals. Clients are encouraged to understand the ways that social constructions of gender have shaped their experience and contributed to the problems that bring them to counseling. Because the client's problems are not just a result of intrapsychic issues, but also a function of societal oppression and gender role limitations, the client is encouraged to create change at both the individual and societal levels.

Brown and Brodsky (1992) outline the following characteristics of feminist therapy:

1. Valuing diversity. Traditional psychotherapies have reflected the experience of white, heterosexual men. Feminist therapy sees women's experience as equally valuable and normative. Differences between women based on race, class, age, religious, and sexual orientation are also respected and brought to the center of the therapeutic process.

2. Attention to power dynamics in the therapeutic relationship. When therapists have more power, it replicates the inequalities of the larger society which have contributed to the client's problems. Power inequalities between therapist and client also work against the goal of empowering the client to create change for themselves.

3. A theory of human behavior which pays attention not only to intrapsychic variables, but also focuses on social/contextual variables. Feminist therapists focus on the impact that gender has on the client's social environment and self-identity.

4. A reliance on the empirical data provided by feminist scholarship on the psychology of women and gender.

5. A belief that all adults should achieve a balance of both healthy autonomy and relational competence, rather than regarding these traits as essential gender differences.

6. Setting therapeutic goals that include a new understanding of the social/cultural realties that impact on client's life, as well as intrapsychic change. The therapeutic focus is on empowering the client to change the social, interpersonal and political environment, rather than adjust to it.

Brooks (2001) describes six core components of the MASTERY model of gender sensitive counseling for working with traditional men.

1. **M**onitor personal reactions to men and male behavior styles. Part of the masculine gender role includes behaviors such as violence, withdrawal, sexism, sexual excess, and drug abuse, to which the therapist may have negative reactions. Such reactions are likely to interfere with the therapeutic process, so the therapist must move beyond these feelings and learn to value the client. Many traditional men are angry or defensive about participating in counseling, so they are especially sensitive to disapproval.

2. **A**ssume male client is feeling pain. Recognize the hurt attached to a masculine gender role which makes men feel like they are not "man enough", expects them to ignore physical and emotional pain, and makes it difficult for them to form deep emotional relationships.

3. **S**ee male client's problems in gender context. Encourage clients to see themselves in a gendered social context. Help them understand the ways that they are products of and sometimes victims of a gendered culture. Many men experience great relief as they recognize that their "failures" are less personal and more a result of a damaging socialization process.

4. **T**ransmit empathy and understanding so that hidden emotional pain can be expressed. Because of masculine gender role socialization it can be especially difficult for men to express painful emotions. Group therapy with other men can help a man feel safer to explore these feelings as they see the struggles that others face. Empathy can also be expressed by a male counselor who shares his own experiences or by a female counselor who shares the experiences she has had with important men in her life.

5. **E**mpower men to change. It is not enough for a client to understand that his behavior is connected to his gender role. He must also be encouraged to change his gender role values and assumptions.

6, **R**espect resistance and **Y**ield some control to larger system. It is important for the therapist to realize that any change that the client attempts may be met with resistance from families and larger social system. Further, while change must occur at both individual and societal level, not all men will take on the larger project of changing the system. Be patient and respect their reluctance, while realizing that change often happens slowly.

References:

Brooks, G.R. (2001). Masculinity and men's mental health. *Journal of American College Health, 49* (6), 285-296.

Brown, L.S. & Brodsky, A.M. (1992). The future of feminist therapy. *Psychotherapy, 29,* 51-57.

Discussion/Activity Suggestions:

1. *ABCs of Gender Activity: Gender and Personal Coping Styles.* The questionnaire in Box 12.3 can be used for a class exercise. Ask students to fill it out anonymously and turn it in. Compile the data and report back to the class. If you have a group that is primarily one gender, you may wish to ask each student to give the questionnaire to someone of the other gender in addition to filling it out for themselves. This will allow for a meaningful comparison of responses. When you report your findings, ask the class if a gender difference in coping with depression was confirmed. What is the significance of coping styles for promoting mental health in men and women?

2. *ABCs of Gender Activity: Gender and Personal Coping Styles.* Box 12.3 describes research on gender differences in coping with depression. Divide students into small groups and ask them to develop a list of coping strategies for dealing with feelings of fear and anxiety. Might there be gender differences in these strategies as well?

3. *Discussion:* Ask students to discuss the following question: "If gender roles were eliminated, what would happen to mental health and mental illness?

4. *Activity: Design a Prevention Program.* Break students into small groups and ask each group to design a program to prevent eating disorders on campus.

Paper Assignment

Cross-Cultural or Multicultural Analysis of Gender and Mental Illness: Ask students to choose one of the disorders discussed in this chapter and conduct a cross-cultural or multicultural comparison of the role gender plays in this disorder. Are the numbers of males and females diagnosed with this disorder the same or different across cultures? Are there similarities or differences in the role gender plays in this disorder across cultures? How is the disorder treated in each culture? Does the treatment take gender into account? What does a cross-cultural or multicultural analysis of this disorder contribute to our understanding of the role gender plays in mental health and mental illness?

InfoTrac Exercises

1. Using the keyword search term **eating disorders** find an article which examines a treatment program. What does this program assume about the causes of eating disorders? Who does the treatment target? How effective is the treatment? Is gender addressed in the treatment? Explain.

2. Using the key word search term **gender and alcohol** find an article which addresses gender differences in alcohol use. What gender differences does the article address? How do these gender differences fit in with the information on gender differences in alcohol use described in the text

Test Bank for Chapter 12

Multiple Choice Questions

1. Explain two traditional concepts that are relevant to understanding the relationship between gender and psychopathology, Obj. 1, p. 263, ans. b

Which theory of mental illness dominated thinking about women until the end of the 19th century?
a. Psychotropic theory
b. Reproductive organ theory
c. Irrationality theory
d. Neurasthenia theory

2. Summarize findings related to gender and ethnic biases and the potential for stereotyping in labeling behavior as psychopathological, Obj. 2, p. 264, ans. c

Psychiatric symptoms are most likely to be reported if
a. the interviewer is a man and the respondent is either male or female.
b. the interviewer is either a man or a woman and the respondent is a female.
c. the interviewer is a woman and the respondent is either male or female.
d. the interviewer is either a man or a woman and the respondent is a male.

3. Summarize findings related to gender and ethnic biases and the potential for stereotyping in labeling behavior as psychopathological, Obj. 2, p. 264, ans. b

Current evidence regarding gender bias in the diagnosis of mental illness reveals that
a. there is no gender bias in the diagnostic process.
b. more pathology is attributed to men described as passive and to women described as aggressive.
c. depressed women are more likely to be diagnosed as having an organic disorder.
d. female psychiatric patients are judged to be more disturbed than male patients.

4. Summarize findings related to gender and ethnic biases and the potential for stereotyping in labeling behavior as psychopathological, Obj. 2, p. 265, ans. a

Research on rates on mental illness in Israel demonstrates:
a. that there are both gender and cultural differences in patterns of psychopathology.
b. that there are cultural differences, but no gender differences in patterns of psychopathology.
c. that there are gender differences, but no cultural differences in patterns of psychopathology.
d. that there are neither cultural nor gender differences in patterns of psychopathology.

5. Summarize findings related to gender and ethnic biases and the potential for stereotyping in labeling behavior as psychopathological, Obj. 2, p. 266, ans. c

Which of the following labels was ultimately not included in DSM-IV?
a. dependent personality disorder
b. premenstrual dysphoric disorder
c. self-defeating personality disorder
d. sexual abuse of adult

6. Summarize findings related to gender and ethnic biases and the potential for stereotyping in labeling behavior as psychopathological, Obj. 2, p. 266, ans. d

Which personality disorder is disproportionately diagnosed in women?
a. paranoid personality disorder
b. restricted personality disorder
c. antisocial personality disorder
d. histrionic personality disorder

7. Summarize findings related to gender and ethnic biases and the potential for stereotyping in labeling behavior as psychopathological, Obj. 2, p. 266, ans. b

Which condition is diagnosed more frequently in males?
a. borderline personality disorder
b. oppositional defiant disorder
c. major depression
d. panic disorder

8. Explain why women have been viewed as more vulnerable to mental disorder and why men have recently become more numerous in psychiatric populations, Obj. 3, p. 267, ans. d

Which of the following is NOT an example of internalizing disorders?
a. panic attacks
b. phobias
c. depression
d. substance abuse

9. Explain why women have been viewed as more vulnerable to mental disorder and why men have recently become more numerous in psychiatric populations, Obj. 3, p. 268, ans. a

Changes in categorization practices now suggest that
a. men have slightly higher rates of mental illness than women.
b. women have slightly higher rates of mental illness than men.
c. men have substantially higher rates of mental illness than women.
d. there is no gender difference in rates of mental illness.

10. Summarize current thinking about gay and lesbian mental health, Obj. 4, p. 269, ans. b

The risk of suicide among gay and lesbian adolescents
a. is no different that the risk for heterosexual adolescents.
b. is significantly greater than for heterosexual adolescents.
c. is significantly less than for heterosexual adolescents.
d. is slightly less than for heterosexual adolescents.

11. Explain the distinction between universally recognized patterns of disordered behavior and culture-bound syndromes, Obj. 5, p. 269, ans. b

The example of Anna and David in the opening vignette illustrates
a. the universality of some forms of mental illness.
b. the influence of culture in constructing concepts of mental illness.
c. cultural commonalties in gendered definitions of mental illness.
d. the tendency for women's disorders to be "internalized" while men's disorders are "externalized."

12. Explain the distinction between universally recognized patterns of disordered behavior and culture-bound syndromes, Obj. 5, p. 270, ans. c

A mental disorder characterized by a man's belief that his penis is retracting into his abdomen is called
a. nervios.
b. dhat syndrome.
c. koro.
d. latah.

13. Explain the distinction between universally recognized patterns of disordered behavior and culture-bound syndromes, Obj. 5, p. 270, ans. a

Which of the following culture-bound syndromes is experienced primarily by women?
a. nervios
b. dhat syndrome
c. windigo psychosis
d. koro

14. Summarize data supporting the notion of eating disorders as a culture-bound syndrome, Obj. 6, p. 271, ans. b

When we look over the history of anorexia, we see that
a. it results from a fear of femininity.
b. it has been explained in a number of different ways.
c. it used to affect men as much as women.
d. it is a relatively recent phenomena.

15. Summarize data supporting the notion of eating disorders as a culture-bound syndrome, Obj. 6, p. 272, ans. d

Eating disorders seem to be related to
a. cultural definitions of femininity.
b. perfectionism.
c. individual control issues.
d. all of the above.

16. Summarize data supporting the notion of eating disorders as a culture-bound syndrome, Obj. 6, p. 273, ans. b

Who is the most likely to develop an eating disorder?
a. an African American working-class woman with a strong racial identity.
b. an upper-class, white woman who is a college student.
c. a poor white woman who has good social support.
d. a white middle-class woman who is a feminist.

17. Summarize data supporting the notion of eating disorders as a culture-bound syndrome, Obj. 6, p. 273, ans. a

Compared to women, men diagnosed with eating disorders
a. are more likely to identify as homosexual or bisexual.
b. are more likely to binge in response to negative emotions.
c. are less likely to be diagnosed with another psychiatric disorder.
d. all of the above

18. Explain the characteristics of transgenderism and tranvestism, Obj. 7, p. 274, ans. c

Transgenderism
a. is more common in women than men.
b. always includes sex reassignment surgery.
c. has no known origin or cause.
d. involves the experience of sexual arousal through cross-dressing.

19. Summarize the factors believed to contribute to the greater incidence of depression among women, Obj. 8, p. 276, ans. d

The most common types of depression
a. are equally prevalent in both genders.
b. are slightly more likely to be experienced by men.
c. are slightly more likely to be experienced by women.
d. are two to four times more likely to be experienced by women.

20. Summarize the factors believed to contribute to the greater incidence of depression among women, Obj. 8, p. 276, ans. c

Which of the following is NOT a risk factor for depression?
a. being female
b. sexual abuse
c. middle class income
d. old age

20. Summarize the factors believed to contribute to greater incidence substance abuse among men, Obj. 9, p. 278, ans. a

Which of the following statements concerning gender differences in substance abuse is FALSE?
a. Depression is more common among alcoholic men than alcoholic women.
b. Alcoholic men are more likely to be regularly employed than alcoholic women.
c. Multiple substance abuse may be more common among women than men.
d. Substance-abusing women are more likely to live with a substance-abusing partner.

21. Summarize the factors believed to contribute to greater incidence substance abuse among men, Obj. 9, p. 278, ans. b

A liver enzyme that helps eliminate alcohol
a. is more active in women.
b. is more active in men.
c. is less active in alcoholics of both genders.
d. is more active in alcoholics of both genders.

22. Summarize the findings regarding the relationship between gender and anxiety disorders, Obj. 10, p. 279, ans. d

Which group is more prone to experience anxiety disorders?
a. middle aged women
b. elderly men
c. middle aged men
d. young women

23. Summarize the findings regarding the relationship between gender and antisocial personality disorder, Obj. 11, p. 280, ans. a

Individuals diagnosed with antisocial personality disorder
a. are more likely to be younger males.
b. experience high levels of anxiety.
c. generally express low levels of sexual desire.
d. all of the above.

24. Summarize the findings regarding the relationship between gender and antisocial personality disorder, Obj. 11, p. 280, ans. d

Antisocial personality disorder
a. is congruent with the masculine gender role.
b. may be underdiagnosed among women.
c. is associated with recurrent job troubles and severe marital problems.
d. all of the above.

25. Summarize the findings regarding gender differences in schizophrenia, Obj. 12, p. 16, ans. b

Compared to men, women who are diagnosed with schizophrenia
a. have higher rates of hospitalization and higher risk of suicide.
b. demonstrate better functioning both before and after diagnosis and treatment.
c. experience earlier onset and more severe symptoms in the first decade.
d. exhibit significantly less cerebral asymmetry.

Short-Answer Questions

26. Why did feminists object when the diagnostic label "self-defeating personality disorder" was suggested for inclusion in DSM-IV?

27. Why might the criteria for "conduct disorder" be sexist?

28. Why are men now a larger percentage of psychiatric hospitalizations?

29. According to the text, why do gay men and lesbians have somewhat higher rates of depression, substance abuse and attempted suicide?

30. Give an example of a culture-bound syndrome (other than eating disorders) which is influenced by gender.

31. What factors provide protection from eating disorders?

32. Define *gender identity disorder.*

33. Why was there little research on women and alcohol until the 1970s?

34. Why might antisocial personality disorder be more common among men than women?

35. Name two gender differences in schizophrenia.

Essay Questions

36. Why have women been overrepresented in psychiatric statistics?

37. What evidence supports the idea that eating disorders are a culture-bound syndrome?

38. Why are women at greater risk for depression?

39. What factors contribute to higher rates of substance abuse among men?

Chapter 13
Gender and the Media

Learning Objectives

1. Define media and briefly explain the factors involved in reading media messages.

2. Explain how media may be said to represent tribal stories, emphasizing how these mediated representations help construct reality and prescribe ideals for members of a society.

3. List and briefly explain nine current issues surrounding gender and the media.

4. Summarize the research findings regarding media and gender socialization, and then explain why the conclusions surrounding this research remain so tentative.

5. List seven points demonstrating that advertisements extend far beyond the mere promotion of products and services, and then connect these points to gender construction and performance.

6. Summarize the contributions of Jean Kilbourne and Erving Goffman to our understanding of gender representations in advertising.

7. Summarize the research findings regarding television as an "educator" in our personal lives.

8. Explain how and why representations of lesbians and gay men in the media have changed.

9. Explain why pornographic media merit special attention in understanding gender representations.

10. List and summarize the findings regarding five other relatively gender-segregated media formats, emphasizing the Internet's potential as a gender-free medium.

Summary

♦ Regardless of its form, all media transmit messages about human experience and ideals. The media are critical agents in gender socialization. Media has an impact on how we experience reality, and the media have great potential for positive or negative influence.

♦ Nine issues surround the relationship between gender and the media on the personal, interpersonal, and cultural levels..

♦ Classic research on the representation of gender across children's media demonstrated a persistent pattern of subordination of girls' abilities and activities compared to those of boys. In general, this pattern still continues.

♦ Relatively high levels of aggression and violence are common in children's media, especially in interactive electronic games. Kafai (1999) offers some useful insights into video game culture. Research conclusions are tentative and problematic regarding the impact of violent models on children's development and actual behavior.

- Magazines and music videos comprise important media formats for teenagers in the West. Gender stereotyping and the derogation of women and women's roles still permeate these media formats.

- Advertising is more than the promotion of goods and services. The work of Jean Kilbourne (1968) and Erving Goffman (1979) began the scientific studies of gender representation in advertising. The patterns identified by these two researchers persist in this medium.

- Television programming often functions as an educator in matters of gender, love, sexuality, and family life. Television offers powerful models and ideals of adolescence, love, courtship, marriage, and family.

- The representation of lesbians and gay men in the media has both increased and changed and become more positive over the last two decades. This community represents an affluent market for media advertisers.

- Some forms of media are relatively segregated by gender. Pornography is an overwhelmingly male medium, and researchers have attempted to determine if the sex and gender messages contained within pornography affect how men treat women and children. Broadcast sports are also a male domain across the globe.

- Soap operas and talk shows constitute overwhelmingly female media domains. Illicit sexuality is a soap opera mainstay, and talk shows blur the boundaries between information and entertainment. Tabloid talk shows normalize very unusual behavior. Popular magazines are typically oriented toward one gender or the other. Although the Internet has potential as a gender-free medium, current trends make this unlikely.

In-Class Activities

Lecture Suggestion:

Lecture: Gay Men on Television

As the text describes, the representation of gay men and lesbians in the mass media has increased and become more positive since the 1970s. An article by Kylo-Patrick Hart describes this change more specifically as it applies to television in the United States:

Hart (2000) describes changes in the representation of gay men in terms of four stages which were originally applied to the portrayal of ethnic minorities on television. During the first stage of **nonrecognition,** the group is invisible. In the second stage, **ridicule**, the group is stereotyped and presented in a farcical manner. The third stage, **regulation**, portrays members of the group as protectors of the existing social order, for example as police officers and detectives. In the final stage, **respect**, group members are shown in the complete range of roles that they occupy in real life. These portrayals can be positive, negative, or even stereotypical, but because there is a diversity of roles, negative roles and stereotypes are not as harmful as they are in earlier stages.

Gay men were in the first stage of nonrecognition on television until the late 1960s. This invisibility was broken by a CBS documentary in 1967 entitled "The Homosexuals," which essentially depicted gay men as unhappy, lonely, promiscuous, and sick. Now visible, gay men moved into the stage of ridicule. Talk shows, dramatic series and comedies made fun of gays and avoided including anything in their programming which might indicate positive support for homosexuality. For example, the show "Laugh-In" was the first network show to regularly feature a supposedly gay man—a stereotypically effeminate character named Bruce who was the butt of a long series of antigay jokes. In a few years the show averaged one joke about gay men or gay liberation per episode.

In the late 1970s, gay men reached the stage of regulation with the introduction of a positive gay male character on the police sitcom "Barney Miller, " and also began to appear in positive roles on other shows. This change coincided with the new awareness of the diversity of gay men's lives brought about by the gay liberation movement, and continued into the early 1980s. However, these strides forward were interrupted in the mid 1980s by the advent of AIDS and its portrayal in the media as "the gay plague." In the late 1980s a number of prime-time shows featured episodes on AIDS, and all of these served to either explicitly or implicitly, link gay men to the disease.

Gay men entered the respect stage in the 1990s. Political changes which gave gay men wider recognition and greater levels of tolerance, were reflected in television shows which portrayed gay men in a variety of roles. In 1990 the show "thirtysomething" had two recurring gay characters who eventually were shown together in bed. In 1992 the daytime soap opera "One Life to Live" featured a story about a gay teenager, and in 1995 the soap "All My Children" introduced several gay characters. By 1997 when "Ellen" came out, gay male characters appeared regularly on shows such as "Chicago Hope," "Frasier," "Roseanne," and "The Simpsons." During the 1998-1999 season, the show "Will and Grace" introduced prime-time television's first gay male lead character.

Although there has been great progress in the representation of gay men of television, there is still room for improvement. For example, gay men have not yet been shown kissing. Hart (2000) cautions that it is not enough just to include gay men in television shows, care must be taken to avoid 1) stereotypical stories about AIDS which imply it is primarily a gay disease, 2) including gay story lines only when there is a negative outcome, 3) reducing diverse gay communities to a single stereotypical lifestyle, and 4) homophobic jokes, plot twists, gay stereotypes and derogatory epithets.

References:

Hart, K.R. (2000). Representing gay men on American television. *The Journal of Men's Studies*, *9* (1), 59-69.

Discussion/Activity Suggestions:

1. *Zoom and Enlarge Activity: Gender on the Global Silver Screen.* Box 13.2 lists some popular films which deal with gender issues. Ask your class to suggest some other films to add to the list, and then request that they watch one of the films either alone or in a small group. Ask them to answer the following questions: What gendered issues did the film deal with? What messages did it convey about traditional gender roles? Did it offer alternatives to traditional gender roles? What lessons were conveyed about gender? Ask them to summarize their analysis of the film in a short review, including a rating of 1 to 5 stars for its portrayal of gender issues. Compile the reviews and make them available as a handout or on a class website.

2. *Slide Show Activity: Gender Representations of the Global Television Screen.* Have your class

examine global gender representations in magazines. Most college libraries carry popular magazines from other countries, or if you have international students in class, ask them to bring in some magazines from their countries. Divide students into small groups and have them examine the magazine ads for gender representation. Use Goffman's five patterns of gender related "behavior displays" to categorize the ads. Encourage them to look for any other notable gender differences as well. When the groups are finished, have them present their findings to the class. Are there cultural differences in gender representations in magazine ads? Do they follow any of the cultural differences described in Box 13.1?

3. *Discussion:* Ask students what their favorite television programs are. What do these shows communicate about gender? Do they perpetuate traditional gender roles, or do they present alternative models for thinking about gender?

4. *Activity: Trends in Fashion Magazines.* Bring fashion magazines into class. Divide students into pairs, and give each pair a magazine. Ask them to find examples of the trends in fashion magazine ads described on p. 293 of the text. Also ask them if there are any ads which seem to be exceptions to these trends. Have students share their examples with the class.

Paper Assignment

Archival Research Project: Ask students to conduct archival research in order to test a hypothesis regarding gender and the media. For example, they might explore gender bias in children's literature or movies, gender roles on television, gender differences in women's and men's magazines, etc. Have them present their research in a poster session which is open to the campus. (You will probably need to meet with students at least once to assist them with their research design.)

InfoTrac Exercise

Using the keyword search term **violence and media**, find an article which discusses the relationship between gender, violence and the media. What role does gender play in this issue? Based on this article, should violence in the media be regulated? Why or why not?

Test Bank for Chapter 13

Multiple Choice Questions

1. Define media and explain the factors involved in reading media messages, Obj. 1, p. 285, ans. b

The process of creating meaning in response to a media messages is called
a. listening to the message.
b. reading the message.
c. media interpretation.
d. mediated meaning.

2. Explain how mediated representations help construct reality, Obj. 2, p. 286, ans. c

Portrayals of crime rates, perpetrators and victims on television
a. are a fairly accurate representation of reality.
b. challenge stereotypes.
c. create the illusion that crime is rampant.
d. give people a false sense of security.

3. Explain nine current issues surrounding gender and the media, Obj. 3, p. 287, ans. c

What does it mean to say that "media presentations offer a hegemonic ideology"?
a. Media are potent agents of gender socialization.
b. Media can normalize the unusual.
c. Media present male dominance as though it is natural and inevitable.
d. Media products are a source of cultural colonialism.

4. Summarize research regarding media and gender socialization, Obj. 4, p. 288, ans. d

Gender stereotyping on children's television
a. is no longer much of a problem.
b. is a problem in advertisements, but not in programming.
c. is a problem in standard programming, but not in educational programming.
d. despite some improvement, continues to be a problem.

5. Summarize research regarding media and gender socialization, Obj. 4, p. 289, ans. b

Which of the following hypotheses regarding media violence and children has the strongest research support?
a. Violent entertainment allows boys to express strong emotions.
b. Children desire arousal.
c. Only aggressive children prefer to watch media violence.
d. Aggression-filled games allow children to come to terms with war, violence, and death.

6. Summarize research regarding media and gender socialization, Obj. 4, p. 290, ans. a

Video games
a. are overwhelmingly a masculine pastime from childhood through college.
b. are somewhat more popular among boys than girls.
c. are much more popular with boys during childhood, but this gender difference subsides in adolescence.
d. are equally enjoyed by males and females at all ages.

7. Summarize research regarding media and gender socialization, Obj. 4, p. 290, ans. d

When children were allowed to create their own video games,
a. boys and girls both preferred teaching games.
b. sports games were the most popular with boys.
c. action games were the least popular with girls.
d. boys and girls both preferred adventure games.

8. Summarize research regarding media and gender socialization, Obj. 4, p. 290, ans. c

Video games created by girls usually contained
a. some conflict between good and evil.
b. very little action.
c. reality-oriented goals.
d. a high level of fantasy.

9. Summarize research regarding media and gender socialization, Obj. 4, p. 291, ans. a

Research on the contents of *Seventeen* magazine revealed
a. substantial changes in the representation of female sexuality.
b. a critical stance toward traditional social roles and interests for teenage girls.
c. the continued presentation of men as sexual agents and women as sexual objects.
d. strong disapproval of homosexuality, oral sex, and masturbation.

10. Summarize research regarding media and gender socialization, Obj. 4, p. 291, ans. b

A study of country music videos found that
a. women were likely to be portrayed as sex objects or sexual predators.
b. male artists were more likely to be portrayed stereotypically than female artists.
c. the number of female artists was equivalent to the number of male artists.
d. there was a high rate of condescending or traditional portrayals of women.

11. List seven points demonstrating that advertisements extend far beyond mere promotion, Obj. 5, p. 292, ans. c

Gender stereotyping
a. has been documented in toy advertisements, but is relatively rare in medical advertising.
b. is common in advertising in the United States, but is unusual in European countries.
c. is found in a variety of product ads, and occurs on a global scale.
d. is prominent in general magazine ads, but fairly uncommon in television advertising.

12. List seven points demonstrating that advertisements extend far beyond mere promotion, Obj. 5, p. 292, ans. a

Advertising is much more than the promotion of goods and services, it also
a. links heart-felt emotions to products and trivializes profound feelings.
b. ignores our cultural and social heritage.
c. minimizes the values and ideology of the target audience.
d. all of the above.

13. Summarize the contributions of Kilbourne and Goffman, Obj. 6, p. 293, ans. b

Which of the following is NOT one of Erving Goffman's "behavior displays"?
a. men are larger or taller than women.
b. men stare off into vacant space rather than looking directly at the viewer.
c. women cradle or caress objects.
d. if there is an activity in the image, men have the active role.

14. Understand gender representation in advertising, Obj. 6, p. 293, ans. b

In facism, women
a. are represented by their faces.
b. are represented by their bodies.
c. are shown looking directly at the observer.
d. are shown staring off into space

15. Understand gender representation in advertising, Obj. 6, p. 293, ans. d

Women in fashion magazine ads
a. are presented in sexualized and demeaning poses.
b. are portrayed as empowered and androgynous.
c. are shown as achievement oriented, yet seductive and sensual.
d. all of the above.

16. Summarize the research regarding television as an "educator," Obj. 7, p. 296, ans. a

Hours spent in television viewing appears correlated with
a. stronger endorsement of recreational sex.
b. lower expectations regarding the sexual activity of peers.
c. more extensive sexual experience, especially for men.
d. all of the above.

17. Summarize the research regarding television as an "educator", Obj. 7, p. 296, ans. a

A central message of current sitcoms is that a happier family life results from
a. gender similarity and equality.
c. greater male dominance.
d. greater female dominance.
d. single parenting.

18. Explain how representations of lesbians and gay men have changed, Obj. 8, p. 297, ans. b

Since the 1970s the representation of gay men and lesbians in the mass media
a. has increased, but continues to be dominated by negative portrayals.
b. has both increased and changed in a more positive direction.
c. has actually decreased, although portrayals are generally more positive.
d. has not significantly changed.

19. Explain how representations of lesbians and gay men have changed, Obj. 8, p. 298, ans. c

As a marketing group, lesbians
a. are younger than gay men.
b. have more education than gay men.
c. do not exhibit the same upscale characteristics as gay men.
d. have more disposable income than gay men.

20. Explain why pornographic media merit special attention in understanding gender representations, Obj. 9, p. 299, ans. c

Most pornographic materials
a. are produced by women for men.
b. are produced by men for heterosexual couples.
c. are produced by men for men.
d. are produced by men for women.

21. Explain why pornographic media merit special attention in understanding gender representations, Obj. 9, p. 301, ans. b

In a recent study of pornography which format was found to have the highest levels of sexual violence against women?
a. magazines
b. Usenet
c. videos
d. there was no difference between formats.

22. Summarize the findings regarding sports media and gender, Obj. 10, p. 301, ans. d

In a study of sports commentary, it was found that_____were referred to by their last names, while _____were referred to by their first names.
a. men of all races, women of all races
b. white men and women, minority men and women
c. men of all races and white women, minority women
d. white men, women and minority men

23. Summarize the findings regarding magazines and gender, Obj. 10, p. 303, ans. c

In man-oriented magazines
a. men are frequently portrayed as spouses or parents.
b. men are shown somewhat more often in occupational roles than in nurturing roles.
c. men are typically depicted as dominant, in control, and involved in unemotional relationships.
d. men are primarily represented with typical physical gender traits.

24. Summarize the findings regarding magazines and gender, Obj. 10, p. 303, ans. b

In a study of the representation of domestic violence in women's magazines, it was found that
a. there was an emphasis on prevention and social change.
b. the role of the abuser and society in domestic violence was ignored.
c. men were blamed and the focus was on changing male behavior.
d. domestic violence was rarely discussed.

25. Summarize the findings regarding the Internet and gender, Obj. 10, p. 304, ans. a

On the Internet,
a. men dominate Usenet and e-mail discussion groups.
b. gender-influenced inequalities have almost been eliminated.
c. women dominate e-mail discussion groups while men dominate Usenet groups.
d. men dominate Usenet groups except those devoted to women and feminism.

Short-Answer Questions

26. Define *media.*

27. Explain media as cultural colonialism.

28. What recommendations would you make to a software company regarding computer games for girls?

29. Why is it difficult to conclude that gender-stereotypical children's media causes later gender-role stereotyping and rigidly gendered behavior?

30. How are men portrayed in advertisements?

31. Describe two of Goffman's gender-related "behavior displays."

32. What messages about sex do adolescents hear when they watch television?

33. Why has the representation of gay men and lesbians in the mass media increased and become more positive?

34. What messages about sex are communicated on soap operas?

35. Is the Internet a gender-free medium? Explain.

Essay Questions

36. What suggestions do you have for making mass media a place where gender equality is promoted?

37. What does advertising communicate about gender?

38. Should violent pornography be made illegal? Why or why not? Use research on pornography to support your position.

Chapter 14
Gender and Power

Learning Objectives

1. Define *power*, and explain the relationship between power and masculinity.

2. Describe the various facets of the relationship between gender and power.

3. Define *sexual harassment*, and summarize the problems in determining the prevalence of this form of coercive power.

4. Describe the important characteristics of harassers and the harassed, and then summarize the various explanations for the occurrence of sexual harassment.

5. Distinguish between rape and sexual assault, and summarize the methodological problems in determining the prevalence of sexual assault.

6. List and explain the types of sexual assault, and summarize the findings regarding the impact of sexual assault.

7. Explain how traditional attitudes toward domestic violence were reflected in two relevant legal principles, and then summarize the accomplishments of feminists in regard to domestic violence.

8. Summarize the controversy surrounding domestic violence as a gendered phenomenon.

9. Summarize current findings regarding the characteristics of batterers and their targets.

10. Briefly summarize the issues related to gender and the legal system.

11. Briefly summarize recent progress in women's access to political power.

12. Briefly summarize the current status of gender equity in the U.S. military.

13. List and explain the current issues related to gender and organized religion.

Summary

♦ The concepts of power and masculinity are closely intertwined. Feminists have provided an analysis of power as a gender-related phenomenon.

♦ Sexual harassment is an unwelcome and repetitive pattern of sex-related behavior that interferes with functioning or well-being. Such illegal behavior appears fairly prevalent in the workplace and academia. Explanations for sexual harassment, including same-sex sexual harassment emphasize overconformity to the masculine role and power relations.

♦ The term *sexual assault* has a broader meaning than rape. Six types of sexual assault have been identified: acquaintance rape, statutory rape, stranger rape, marital rape, male rape, and gang rape. Sexual assault is physically and psychologically traumatic. Current explanations for sexual assault emphasize socialization for a predatory masculine sexuality.

♦ Domestic violence is the physical abuse of an intimate partner. It is ensconced in traditional ideas about marriage and masculine privilege. Legal reforms and grassroots social programs have provided greater protection for battered women. Batterers overadhere to notions of masculine power in relationships. Battered women tolerate abuse for a number of socioeconomic reasons.

♦ Around the world, legal systems continue to represent entrenched masculine power. Women have made considerable progress in gaining power in the various aspects of the legal system in North America.

♦ Political power remains a resolutely masculine domain all over the world. Gender stereotypes influence the perception of political leaders. The gradual entry of women into international leadership is slowly changing the perception of certain gendered cultural practices as crimes and issues of human rights.

♦ In most societies, the warrior role is a masculine pursuit. The U.S. military is the most ethnically integrated institution and continues to undergo a process of gender integration. There are many cogent and convincing arguments both for and against a fully gender-integrated military.

♦ Organized religion is a powerful force in the social construction of gender. Four themes describe the relationship between gender and power in organized religion around the world.

In-Class Activities

Lecture Suggestion:

Lecture: Men and Rape Responsibility

The text makes the point that most programs designed to prevent sexual assault focus on self-defense and safety advice for women, and that few efforts are made to change the behavior of men. You may wish to address this issue in class. In a review of feminist contributions to the understanding of rape, Patricia Rozee and Mary Koss outline what a rape prevention program that targets men should look like:

Rape prevention programs are most effective when they are conducted with male-only groups. Men are more likely to get defensive in mixed-sex groups, and such groups may actually promote an adversarial understanding of gender differences, something which is associated with the inclination to rape. Male-only groups promote feelings of safety and may make it more possible for men to be open and honest about their beliefs and actions around sexual aggression.

Rozee and Koss argue that these programs should be based on known cognitive, emotional and behavioral indicators for rape behavior. These include factors associated with power: power motivation and power-sex association, hostility toward women, masculine ideology, conversational domineeringness, and high dominance, as well as factors associated with sexual practices: preference for impersonal sex, callused sexual beliefs, beliefs that female resistance is merely token, personal responsibility, and emulating pornography.

In addition, these programs should challenge the idea that "miscommunication" is the cause of rape. This hypothesis has not been supported by research. As a rule, researchers have found a remarkable level of consistency in the cues that men and women use and interpret as consent. Further, 70 percent of rape victim-survivors fight back physically, which is a fairly clear indicator of lack of consent. In addition, the majority of rape cases are not preceded by consensual sex play. Men who report that they have engaged in sexually aggressive behavior are significantly more likely to "misperceive" than other men or women. The more frequently college men misperceived women's sexual intentions the more frequently they committed sexual assault. Token resistance has been found to be something that both men and women use, and in fact there is some evidence than men practice it more than women do. Actual resistance tends to occur early in the dating process while token resistance is more likely after a significant number of dates. Again, as with misperception, men who are higher in rape beliefs were more likely to interpret a woman's behavior as token resistance. Men who rape tend to see forced sex as really not that wrong. In one study, 84 percent of men who admitted to behavior that met the legal definition of rape, said that what they did was definitely not rape.

Rozee and Koss suggest a program for men based on the principles of Ask, Acknowledge, and Act (AAA). In this method men are told that there is one way to be sure if a woman wants sex or not, and that is to ask. This asking should be begin with the man himself: Is this woman capable of saying yes or no? Is she under the age of consent? Is she too much under the influence or drugs, alcohol, unconscious, or mentally impaired? Are you with someone who does not have a romantic relationship with you, who has not given you the impression that sexual advances would be welcome? If answer is yes to any of these questions, the man should acknowledge that asking for sex is inappropriate and he should then act and stop his initiating behavior. If answer is no to these questions, then the man should ask the woman if she wants to have sex. If she says no, he needs to acknowledge her response, respect her wishes, and act accordingly—stop initiating sex. If she says yes, then he can proceed with a clear conscience.

References:

Rozee, P.D. & Koss, M.P. (2001). Rape: A century of resistance. *Psychology of Women Quarterly, 25* (4) 295-311.

Discussion/Activity Suggestions:

1. *Zoom and Enlarge Activity: A Tale of Two Women.* Box 14.3 tells the story of a man in a powerful position who mentored two women: his daughter, and one of his students. Ask the women in your class if any of them have been mentored by a man either in the private or public sphere. Ask them to share some specifics of how that man was helpful to them

2. *Activity: Sexual Harassment and Assault Programs on Campus.* Ask students to find out what the policies and programs are on campus for reducing incidents of sexual harassment and sexual assault. Alternatively, you could ask someone from the appropriate office to come in and tell your class about these policies and programs. Ask the class if these policies and programs are adequate: Do they address the issue of male power? What do they assume about the causes of sexual harassment and sexual assault? Do they put most of the responsibility for prevention in the hands of women? What recommendations would students make to improve these policies and programs?

3. *Slide Show Activity: A Global Perspective on Domestic Violence.* Box 14.1 describes the status of domestic violence in several countries. Ask your students to get on the Internet and find out about domestic violence in a country not listed here. Have them report their findings to the class.

4. *Discussion:* Ask students to debate the claim that women politicians represent women's interests better than do men.

Paper Assignment

An Analysis of Gendered Power: Assign students the task of analyzing gendered power in one of the institutions in which they participate (e.g., their family, college, workplace, religious organization.) They should look at the hierarchy and governance of the institution, its laws, customs and practices, the way money decisions are made, who has the greatest influence on decisions, what kinds of activities each person or type of person does in the institution, etc. What would change in the institution if power was equally divided between women and men?

InfoTrac Exercises

1. Using one of the keyword search terms **sexual assault**, **sexual harassment**, or **domestic violence**, find an article which describes a program to treat or prevent this type of coercive power. What does the program assume about the causes or consequences of sexual assault, sexual harassment, or domestic violence? How does the treatment or prevention program attempt to deal with these causes or consequences? Has the program been successful? Would you like to see such a program in your community? Why or why not?

2. Find two articles using the keyword search term **power and masculinity**. How is power defined in each of these articles? Are the definitions similar? What connection is drawn between power and masculinity in each article? Do these analyses tie in with the discussion on power and masculinity in the text? Explain.

Test Bank for Chapter 14

Multiple Choice Questions

1. Define *power* and explain the relationship between power and masculinity, Obj. 1, p. 307, ans. d

Power is
a. the ability to influence what happens in interactions.
b. the ability to limit access to resources.
c. the ability to define experiences for others.
d. all of the above

2. Define *power* and explain the relationship between power and masculinity, Obj. 1, p. 307, ans. c

In everyday interactions, dominance behavior elicits
a. negative evaluations of both women and men.
b. negative evaluations of men, but not of women.
c. negative evaluations of women, but not of men.
d. positive evaluations of both women and men.

3. Describe the various facets of the relationship between gender and power, Obj. 2, p. 308, ans. a

Where are women most likely to experience male violence?
a. in their homes
b. in the workplace
c. in public spaces such as parking lots and deserted streets
d. in bars

4. Describe the various facets of the relationship between gender and power, Obj. 2, p. 309, ans. c

Which of the following statements about gender and violence is FALSE?
a. Domestic violence is more likely in patriarchal societies.
b. Women are often blamed for men's violence.
c. Women are generally passive recipients of male violence.
d. In many societies, violence is a way of demonstrating masculinity.

5. Define *sexual harassment* and summarize the problems in determining the prevalence of this form of coercive power, Obj. 3, p. 309, ans. d

When it comes to defining behavior as sexual harassment,
a. men tend to base their perceptions on the perpetrator's behavior.
b. men and women have similar perceptions.
c. women tend to base their perceptions on the target's reactions.
d. women tend to base their perceptions on the perpetrator's behavior.

6. Define *sexual harassment* and summarize the problems in determining the prevalence of this form of coercive power, Obj. 3, p. 309, ans. d

A typical estimate of the prevalence of sexual harassment experience is
a. 25 percent of both women and men.
b. 90 percent of women and 40 percent of men.
c. 85 percent of women and 5 percent of men.
d. 50 percent of women and 15 percent of men.

7. Describe the characteristics of harassers and the harassed, Obj. 4, p. 311, ans. c

Which of the following women is most likely to be sexually harassed?
a. a married woman with a high school education who has a previous history of victimization.
b. a divorced woman who is independently wealthy.
c. a single college educated woman who is very dependent on her job.
d. a married woman with a college education who has financial need.

8. Describe the characteristics of harassers and the harassed, Obj. 4, p. 311, ans. d

Men who harass
a. are likely to be unmarried.
b. typically harass only one woman.
c. tend to have high self-esteem.
d. are often surprised that their attentions are not welcomed.

9. Summarize explanations for the occurrence of sexual harassment, Obj. 4, p. 311, ans. b

A man is more likely to sexually harass if
a. he rejects traditional masculine sexual scripts.
b. his supervisor ignores sexually harassing behaviors.
c. he works in a gender-integrated job.
d. all of the above.

10. Summarize the problems in determining the prevalence of sexual assault, Obj. 5, p. 312, ans. a

Estimating the prevalence of sexual assault
a. has been problematic.
b. has been fairly straightforward.
c. has not been seen as important.
d. has been too complicated to attempt.

11. Explain the types of sexual assault, Obj. 6, p. 313, ans. b

The most common type of adult sexual assault is
a. marital rape.
b. date rape.
c. stranger rape.
d. statutory rape.

12. Explain the types of sexual assault, Obj. 6, p. 313, ans. b

Which of the following characteristics is NOT typical of a rapist?
a. Rapists know their targets and plan their attacks.
b. Rapists are psychiatrically disturbed.
c. Rapists believe the target wanted and enjoyed the sexual encounter.
d. Rapists tend to be domineering and self-centered.

13. Summarize the findings regarding the impact of sexual assault, Obj. 6, p. 314, ans. c

Recognition of rape as a global human rights issue
a. has finally been accomplished.
b. occurred about ten years ago.
c. has been slow.
d. was rapid once it was addressed by the United Nations.

14. Explain traditional attitudes toward domestic violence and summarize the accomplishments of feminists, Obj. 7, p. 315, ans. d

Traditional psychological and sociological literature blamed battering on
a. gendered power differences.
b. gender differences in violence socialization.
c. economic inequality.
d. individual psychopathology.

15. Explain traditional attitudes toward domestic violence and summarize the accomplishments of feminists, Obj. 7, p. 316, ans. a

Mandatory arrest policies for batterers in urban areas of the United States
a. have reduced domestic violence incidents in some areas but not others.
b. have been extremely effective in reducing domestic violence when enforced.
c. have not had a significant impact on domestic violence rates.
d. have actually increased domestic violence rates.

16. Explain traditional attitudes toward domestic violence and summarize the accomplishments of feminists, Obj. 7, p. 317, ans. b

Looking at the problem of domestic violence around the world, we find
a. there has been significant progress.
b. that progress is very slow and uneven.
c. that nothing has changed.
d. a moderate and steady rate of progress.

17. Summarize the current findings regarding the characteristics of batterers and their targets, Obj. 9, p. 317, ans. b

Which of the following is NOT characteristic of men who batter?
a. They blame their victims for what has happened.
b. They brag about what they do to their partners.
c. They minimize and deny their violent actions.
d. The see battering as a way to "show who is the boss."

18. Summarize the current findings regarding the characteristics of batterers and their targets, Obj. 9, p. 318, ans. d

Women may endure domestic violence because
a. they love their partner and believe they can stop the violence.
b. they believe they caused the violence and that their experience is not unusual.
c. they are unable to economically provide for a family.
d. all of the above.

19. Summarize the issues related to gender and the legal system, Obj. 10, p. 319, ans. c

What nation does not permit women to vote?
a. Ukraine
b. Kenya
c. Kuwait
d. Morocco

20. Summarize the issues related to gender and the legal system, Obj. 10, p. 319, ans. a

Which of the following factors is currently hindering women's success in the field of law?
a. the work ethic at law firms.
b. difficulties with being admitted to law school.
c. lack of employment opportunities for women.
d. women's lack of interest in the profession.

21. Summarize the issues related to gender and the legal system, Obj. 10, p. 320, ans. a

What percentage of the incarcerated population are women?
a. 7.5%
b. 23%
c. 42.5%
d. 2%

22. Briefly summarize recent progress in women's access to political power, Obj. 11, p. 321, ans. d

The public appears to want a president's wife to be
a. a government leader who is involved in policymaking.
b. primarily a social leader who presides over ceremonial functions.
c. involved in whatever areas of government she feels are appropriate.
d. active only on "soft" issues such as children, education and health.

23. Briefly summarize recent progress in women's access to political power, Obj. 11, p. 322, ans. d

Women political leaders are viewed as
a. agents of change.
b. more practical, honest and hardworking.
c. less knowledgeable on defense and crime.
d. all of the above.

24. Briefly summarize current status of gender equity in the U.S. military, Obj. 12, p. 324, ans. a

Currently in the U.S. military,_____positions in the Air Force and Army are open to women.
a. almost all
b. all
c. most
d. some

25. Briefly summarize current status of gender equity in the U.S. military, Obj. 12, p. 325, ans. c

A study of a fully gender-integrated unit of peacekeepers in Bosnia revealed
a. no difference in the pregnancy rate when compared to other U.S. military stations in Europe.
b. slightly less military effectiveness and lower troop morale.
c. no differences in performance and war-fighting spirit.
d. significant problems with sexual attractions and relationships.

26. Explain current issues related to gender and organized religion, Obj. 13, p. 325, ans. b

Religious traditions
a. have little influence on the gender ideology of a society.
b. both influence and reflect the gender ideology of a society.
c. are usually contradictory to the gender ideology of a society.
d. reflect a society's gender system, but do not contribute to its maintenance.

27. Explain current issues related to gender and organized religion, Obj. 13, p. 328, ans. b

In general, the more institutionalized a religion becomes,
a. the more equitable is the gender balance in the significant roles of that tradition.
b. the more women are excluded from positions of authority and power.
c. the more likely women are to be ordained.
d. the more likely men are to be relegated to the periphery.

Short-Answer Questions

28. Explain why sexual harassment is a form of coercive power.

29. Describe some of the effects sexual harassment has on people who are harassed.

30. How does a highly gender-segregated workplace contribute to sexual harassment?

31. What cognitive distortions are typical of sex offenders?

32. Why is it problematic to estimate the prevalence of sexual assault?

33. Describe the legal doctrine of *couverture*.

34. What effect is repeated violence likely to have on a target's thinking?

35. Why is a gender balance in elected office important?

36. What gender ideology links men with war and women with peace?

37. Explain the statement "across cultures, established religions depend mightily on the religiosity of women to continue," (p. 328).

Essay Questions

36. What are the difficulties in defining what behavior constitutes sexual harassment?

37. Given the explanations for sexual harassment described in the text, what recommendations would you make if you were a consultant to a workplace that was trying to put an end to sexual harassment?

38. Is domestic violence a gender-related phenomenon? Why or why not?

39. Given the reasons that women stay in abusive relationships, what changes do you see as necessary to make it possible for women to leave such relationships?

40. Should the military be gender-integrated? Why or why not?

Chapter 15
Gender and the Future

Summary

♦ Through the use of questions this chapter asks the reader to project into the future and think about what might happen with the various gendered trends and patterns which were discussed in earlier chapters. Readers are asked to consider what the impact of gender, gender relations and gender roles may have on their personal future and the future of their interpersonal relations. They are also asked to think about gender on the social and global levels, addressing the question of AIDS, sexual violence, education, work, media, physical and mental health. What would the world be like if there was gender equity? The chapter concludes with a brief consideration of gendered issues which were not explored in the text.

In-Class Activities

Lecture Suggestion:

Lecture: Gender and Environmentalism

The text lists a set of topics which were not covered due to space and time considerations. One of the topics is gender and environmentalism. If you would like to devote a little time to this issue, an article by Lynnette Zelezny, Poh-Pheng Chua and Christina Aldrich examines current findings:

A review and meta-analysis of the literature on gender differences in proenvironmental behavior found that overall, women reported greater participation in proenvironmental behavior. Zelezny, Chua and Aldrich propose that this is due to gender role socialization. Across cultures, females are socialized to be more other-directed, more compassionate, nurturing, interdependent and cooperative, while males are socialized to be more independent and competitive. They argue that these qualities lead to greater concern for the environment. A model of ecological value orientations developed by researchers Stern and Dietz, proposes three orientations to environmental issues which motivate individual behavior: the egocentric orientation, which focuses on concern for self (e.g., buying organic food because it affects the individual's health), the anthropocentric orientation, which focuses on concern for other beings (e.g., buying organic food because it affects their children's health), and the ecocentric orientation, which focuses concern on the biosphere (e.g., buying organic food because it improves the soil and reduces pollution.) Research has found that women have stronger beliefs than men in all three of these orientations and that these beliefs predict more proenvironmental behavior.

In a series of three studies designed to examine the impact of gender and gender role socialization on environmental attitudes and behavior, Zelezny, Chua, and Aldrich focus on the ecocentric orientation, because they feel that it reflects an extended "other" viewpoint characteristic of feminine socialization. The first study examined gender differences in environmental behavior and attitudes in childhood and found that for primary and secondary students, girls reported stronger proenvironmental responses on all of the environmental variables (including those designed to measure an ecocentric orientation) in the study than boys. This gender difference in proenvironmentalism then, begins in childhood and is not simply a consequence of motherhood and the desire to protect children against environmental threats, as has been argued by some theorists. In the second study, gender differences in environmental attitudes and behaviors were examined cross-culturally in 14 countries (United States, Canada, Colombia, Costa Rica, the Dominican Republic, Ecuador, El Salvador, Mexico, Panama, Paraguay, Peru, Spain, and Venezuela.) As a group, across all fourteen countries, females reported significantly stronger environmental attitudes and proenvironmental behaviors (again, including measures of ecocentric orientation). A third study was designed to examine the role of socialization in producing these gender differences in environmental attitudes and behaviors. It was found that females had higher levels of socialization to be other oriented and socially responsible. In addition, Zelezny, Chua, and Aldrich make the point that the gender differences in ecocentrism found in the first two studies also provides indirect support for socialization theory, in that ecocentrism represents an "other" orientation.

The authors conclude with some speculation about the future of environmental theory, social action, and policy. They argue that future models of environmentalism will include gender and that as a group, females will be a significant force in environmental activism, policy development, and leadership.

References:

Zelezny, L.C., Chua, P. & Aldrich, C. (2000). Elaboration on gender differences in environmentalism. *Journal of Social Issues, 56* (3), 443-457.

Discussion/Activity Suggestions:

1. *ABCs of Gender Activity: The Gender Environment of Your Everyday Life.* Box 15.2 asks students to list the gender of a wide variety of people in their lives. Ask them to fill it out, and answer the questions "Does the gender distribution of these individuals reflect anything about your attitudes, beliefs, values, and concerns regarding gender?" and "Are there categories you wish you had a different answer for?" Break the class into small groups and ask them to share what they learned from this exercise. You may also wish to collect the surveys and compile the results for the class.

2. *Discussion:* Ask students to speculate about what may happen to the study of gender in the future. Will classes like this one still exist? Why or why not? If they will still exist, what issues will be addressed? If gender relations change, how might classroom interactions be impacted?

3. *Discussion:* As a concluding exercise, go around the room and have each student (and yourself!) answer the following questions: What is something you learned from the class that you would like other people to know? What was something in the class that made you angry? What is a gender-related change you would like to see happen?

Paper Assignment

Gender and the Future: Ask students to write a paper which addresses some of the questions in this last chapter. What is their vision for the future? Encourage them to go beyond their personal future and consider what changes might be possible in their community, their country, and the world as a whole. Ask them to conclude by considering the Marian Wright Edelman quote at the end of the chapter. What does this quote mean for the future of gender and their own lives?

InfoTrac Exercise

Find an article using one of keyword search terms **gender and music**, **gender and art**, **gender and sport**, or **gender and international development**. These are issues which were not covered in the text. What does the article tell you about the role of gender in this issue? Does it tie into any of the areas that were discussed in the text? How? Do you feel that the text should have addressed this issue? Why or why not?

Test Bank for Chapter 15

Multiple Choice Questions

1. Consider the role of gender in your personal future, p. 332, ans. b

When it comes to your personal future,
a. regardless of gender, you can choose freely from among a whole array of life options.
b. your choices are influenced by gendered traditions, social norms, and economic and political realities.
c. gender-related factors are not an issue if you live in a post-industrial society.
d. gender is likely to influence your interpersonal relations, but not other areas of your life.

2. Consider the role of gender in your personal future, p. 333, ans. d

If you have an egalitarian intimate relationship you will likely have
a. fewer time-consuming negotiations.
b. less conflict and easier communication.
c. fewer problems with issues that involve power or priorities.
d. a more exciting relationship which will require much more conscious effort.

3. Describe the current status of legal protection for gay and lesbian families, p. 334, ans. a

The state which permits civil unions between gay men and lesbians is
a. Vermont.
b. California.
c. Minnesota.
d. Massachusetts.

4. Describe the current status of HIV/AIDS, p. 335, ans. c

Which nation has the largest number of people living with HIV in the world?
a. United States
b. India
c. South Africa
d. Zimbabwe

5. Describe the issues surrounding gender and work in postindustrial societies, p. 336, ans. d

To create a wider range of occupations for both women and men, we must
a. stop equating adequate masculinity with monetary achievement.
b. encourage women to become skilled in technology.
c. broaden educational pathways for both genders.
d. all of the above.

Short-Answer Questions

6. What factors make it difficult to provide treatment to HIV-positive individuals in African nations?

7. Explain the role of *technology* and *meaningfulness* in creating gendered limits to education and work.

8. Why is the traditional gender occupational hierarchy likely to continue being reproduced in the developing world?

9. What is a question you have regarding gender which has not been answered by the text?

Essay Questions

10. Write your own "Encounter with Gender" scenario of gender roles in the future.

11. Do you agree with the author of the text that "change toward greater egalitarianism between the genders is more desirable than change in the other direction?" Why or why not?